Songs of the Saints

Enriching our singing by
learning from the songs of Scripture

MIKE RAITER & ROB SMITH

matthiasmedia

SYDNEY · YOUNGSTOWN

Matthias Media
(St Matthias Press Ltd ACN 067 558 365)
Email: info@matthiasmedia.com.au
Internet: www.matthiasmedia.com.au
Please visit our website for current postal and telephone contact information.

Matthias Media (USA)
Email: sales@matthiasmedia.com
Internet: www.matthiasmedia.com
Please visit our website for current postal and telephone contact information.

ISBN 978 1 922206 17 6

Cover design and typesetting by Lankshear Design.

Dedicated to my late father, Bruce Smith, who taught me to love music of many kinds and, most of all, the songs of the saints.

RS

To Joel, Nathan, Pippa and Lauren, who give me more reasons to sing.

MR

Contents

The power of the song

> I plainly judge, and do not hesitate to affirm, that except for theology there is no art that could be put on the same level with music, since except for theology it alone produces what otherwise only theology can do, namely, a calm and joyful disposition.[1]
>
> *Martin Luther*

Just reflect for a moment on how powerful music, and particularly songs, can be—even in the normal course of daily life. Why, for example, is playing at home an advantage in any sport's contest? In part, it is because of the cheering and the singing of the partisan fans. This often-raucous choir lifts the energy and commitment level of the players to the extent that some can even play through incredible pain barriers to win.

Or think about music's well-established ability to

1   M Luther, 'Letter to Louis Senfl' (1530), in J Pelikan and HT Lehmann (eds), *Luther's Works* (55 vols; trans. CM Jacobs; rev. EW Gritsch; Concordia/Fortress, Saint Louis/Philadelphia, 1955-86), vol. 49, pp. 427-8.

relax us—slowing the heart rate, lowering blood pressure, reducing anxiety and decreasing levels of cortisol (the 'stress hormone'). It is also known to relieve boredom, improve concentration, increase morale and even reduce crime. Why else is music played in homes, hospitals, workplaces, shopping centres and on public transport?

Or ponder the role of music in human society. Changes in music both reflect and effect changes in culture. The messages of the songs we listen to have a profound moral impact upon us. It is not without reason that Bob Dylan and the Beatles have been called modern-day prophets. They significantly influenced a whole generation, and they did it through their songs. Music and song have the power to shape a people.

The day a Philistine was slain

Some years ago Mike went to watch his 16-year-old son perform on the saxophone in a 'Gala Concert' that was part of his school's annual music festival. The school has a brass band, a couple of choirs, and a full symphony orchestra. The music tends to be traditional and classical. However, the program also included a performance of the theme from *Mission Impossible*, we suspect as a bit of musical compromise to keep the cultural philistines amongst the parents —like Mike—happy.

At this point we confess that Mike, having grown up in Liverpool (England) in the 1960s, and so nursed not on milk but the Merseybeat, has never developed a musical appetite for anything stronger. While some are transported to heaven by a Brandenburg Concerto, he'd rather go flying with Lucy in the Sky with Diamonds. In short, while Mike likes to support his son, he usually spent a good deal of time at these concerts checking his watch and calculating how many more items he was going to have to endure until released on parole. But that night was different.

The quality of the performances was exceptional, and some of the music they chose to perform was memorable. But the finale was unforgettable. It was Rossini's *William Tell Overture*. It was simply exhilarating. Of course, if you're Mike's vintage whenever you hear this piece of music you can't help but visualize The Lone Ranger galloping across the plain with his faithful Indian companion, Tonto, riding obediently beside him (if you're not a Baby Boomer and haven't a clue what we're talking about, ask your parents). To sit there while an 85-piece orchestra belted out this soul-stirring piece of music was to be lifted from the earthly plane to another stratosphere. It was to momentarily forget where you were and to be taken in your imagination somewhere else. After rapturous applause, the conductor performed parts of the piece again as an encore, this time inviting the heretofore submissively silent audience to release their inhibitions and enthusiastically clap along with the music until their hands began to ache. At the last note, the entire audience rose as one in a standing ovation. And, even Mike, a proud and unabashed musical barbarian stood there, caught along with all the rest, in the thrilling and exhilarating emotion of the moment.

Such is the power of music—even without words.

Songs that stir the saints

Among the people of God, the ability of music and song to lift one's mood or calm a troubled soul is nothing new. When Israel's King Saul was depressed, morose, and inconsolable, it was only the soothing playing of the lyre and the melodious singing of David that brought any relief to his troubled mind (1 Sam 16:23). When David, the now anointed but not yet appointed king of Israel, was at one time trapped in his house, Saul sent men to watch the house and, when the opportunity arose, to kill him. With the odds against him, David found comfort and strength in a song he wrote:

> For behold, they lie in wait for my life...
>
> Each evening they come back,
>   howling like dogs
>   and prowling about the city.
> They wander about for food
>   and growl if they do not get their fill.
>
> *But I will sing of your strength;*
>   *I will sing aloud of your steadfast love in the morning.*
> *For you have been to me a fortress*
>   *and a refuge in the day of my distress.*
>   (Ps 59:3a, 14-16)

God's people have often drawn strength from the power of godly songs. If music by itself is powerful, how much more is truth set to music? Puritan separatist and *Mayflower* pilgrim Edward Winslow described a gathering of fellow-Puritans on the night before they were to set sail for

America in 1620. What lay before them was a dangerous voyage and an unknown future. He recalled that the brethren gathered at the pastor's house for a meal, "where we refreshed ourselves, after tears, with singing of psalms, making joyful melody in our hearts, as well as with the voice... indeed, it was the sweetest melody that ever mine ears heard".[2]

On January 8th, 1956, Jim Elliot and four other young missionaries landed their plane in the heart of Auca Indian territory in Ecuador. For months they had tried to make contact with this remote tribe of cannibals. The story of their martyrdom is now famous. According to Jim's wife, Elizabeth, the night before they left they sang a hymn together:

> We go in faith, our own great weakness feeling,
> And needing more each day thy grace to know,
> Yet from our hearts a song of triumph pealing,
> We rest on thee, and in thy name we go.[3]

Millions of black Africans enslaved in Europe and, particularly, North America expressed their longing for emancipation in spiritual songs of hope. Harking back to Israel's captivity in Egypt, many of these 'spirituals' utilized the theme of crossing the Jordan, marking the exodus from a life of bondage into a new world of freedom. They believed that, just as God saw the sufferings of his people in Egypt and delivered them, so he would bring

2   E Winslow, 'How the Pilgrims Sailed from Delft Haven', 1646; cited in WC Martyn, *The Pilgrim Fathers of New England: A History*, American Tract Society, New York, 1867, p. 74.
3   EG Cherry, 'We Rest on Thee', 1895.

an end to their suffering if they put their hope in him. They would be set free from the chains of slavery and, ultimately, enter into the paradise that awaited them in the age to come:

> Swing low, sweet chariot,
> Coming for to carry me home.
> I looked over Jordan and what did I see,
> Coming for to carry me home,
> A band of angels coming after me,
> Coming for to carry me home.[4]

Throughout history, when God's people have faced overwhelming odds, and have understood that their refuge and strength is in God alone, they've expressed their fears and strengthened their faith not only in words of prose but in songs of worship.

Such is the power of the song.

The devil takes flight...

It is not only the people of God who have understood the power of the song—songs that speak of God, his glories, his promises and his saving works. The devil himself also knows this power—and detests it!

Baptist pastor and writer John Piper recalls over 20 years ago being called to an apartment where there was a woman who was thought to be demon possessed. He went with his assistant. Some other Christian women were there and for two hours they talked to the oppressed

---

4   W Willis, 'Swing Low, Sweet Chariot', 1840.

woman, reading the Scriptures to her and praying prayers of deliverance. Still, she became increasingly violent. She knocked the Bible out of Piper's hand, grabbed the prayer sheets, and shoved him away. Piper recalls that at about one in the morning, when the conflict between Satan and the word of God was at fever pitch, someone in the group began to sing, and others joined in. The effect was dramatic. The woman began to tremble and threaten them if they didn't stop. Then she threw herself on the floor and screamed for Satan not to leave her. Finally, she went into convulsions and then went limp. Later, when she awoke, she remembered nothing of what had happened and was willing to read the Scriptures and pray. Piper concludes that Satan hates the songs of God's people and does what he can to keep a church from being a singing church.[5]

Martin Luther wrote, "The devil takes flight at the sound of music, just as he does at the words of theology."[6]

...but the devil sneaks in

If it is true that Satan detests the singing of God's people, it is also true that he knows how to manipulate its power for his malevolent ends. It has been said, and with some justification, that the devil often enters the church through the choir stalls—or the music team. I'm sure you've heard the joke: What's the difference between a terrorist and a church organist? Answer: you can negotiate

5   J Piper, 'Ambushing Satan with a Song', *Desiring God*, 20 January 1985 (viewed 10 October 2016): www.desiringgod.org/messages/ambushing-satan-with-song

6   M Luther, 'Letter to Louis Senfl' (1530), *Luther's Works*, vol. 49, pp. 427-8.

with a terrorist. Very funny unless, of course, you happen to be the church organist!

In the hands of the unscrupulous, music can corrupt. If it can soothe the troubled breast, it can also seduce the vulnerable heart. If it can inspire the saints to endure suffering for Jesus' sake, it can mould and manipulate vast crowds to commit themselves to political philosophies that are cruel and dehumanizing. If it can serve to teach and encourage the people of God, it can also become a god itself, an idol that promises to give people's lives meaning and purpose. If it can nourish the hearts of God's people, it can feed the ego of the performer masquerading as a minister.

It follows then that, since singing is so potent, we must be very careful to whom we entrust this power. We ought to be very nervous when churches call on people to put their hands up and volunteer for music ministry, particularly if it is a ministry of music leadership. We wouldn't call for volunteers to be put on the preaching roster, nor should we call on volunteers to be the congregation's 'other preachers'—but more of that later. In the hands of the unprincipled, self-serving, immature or undiscerning, music ministry can distract, weaken, and even split a church. But when used by the godly and the wise, the gifted and mature it is a great source for good. Such is the power of the song.

Drinking from the musical well

We have written this book because we believe in the power of congregational singing. We believe in it because we are persuaded it is a good gift of God that conveys many spiritual blessings to his people. When this gift is foolishly abused it can cause incredible damage to the health and unity of a church. But when its power is wisely employed it brings vitality and maturity to the life of a congregation.

We have also written this book because we're discouraged. We're discouraged because in some circles Christians seem to have forgotten the important place singing has in the life of the church. They've forgotten that, unless one is a remarkably gifted ventriloquist, singing requires the opening of the mouth. Too many modern 'worshippers' stand stony-faced and close-mouthed during the songs. And we're discouraged because in some other circles, Christians love to sing, and seem happy to sing anything as long as it mentions 'the Lord' and 'worship' and has a catchy melody. Well, actually, sometimes you don't even need to worry about the melody. We long to see the church passionate *and* discerning about the songs we sing.

The lack of enthusiasm for congregational singing in too many churches is a conundrum. It is a conundrum, as we'll see, given all that the Bible has to say about the topic. But it is perplexing also when one considers that evangelicalism is the deep well from which so much Christian singing has sprung. It sprang from men and women with fine theological minds and spiritually passionate hearts.

Men like Isaac Watts (1674-1748). What an amazing man! Plagued by illness for much of his life, he was blessed with a massive intellect. He had learned Latin by the age of 4, Greek at 9, French at 11, and Hebrew at 13. As a working pastor, he wrote major works on metaphysics, philosophy, logic and astronomy.

And he wrote hymns. Mind you, while he was growing up hymns weren't sung in English churches. The
common practice was to only sing the psalms. Accounts
vary as to how Watts came to write his first hymn, but it
seems he was heard to complain about the paucity of good
songs for churches to sing. He was asked, then, to write
something better, and he penned 'Behold the Glories of
the Lamb Amidst the Father's Throne'. Watts was to write
about 700 more, including, 'When I Survey the Wondrous
Cross', 'Joy to the World', 'Alas! and Did My Saviour Bleed',
'Jesus Shall Reign Where'er the Sun' and 'O God, Our Help
in Ages Past'.[7]

For all his incredible intellectual gifts, Watts knew that
God was to be loved with both the mind and the heart.
And so he wrote and so he sang. All because God had
seized his heart:

Were the whole realm of nature mine,
That were an offering far too small.
Love so amazing, so divine,
Demands my life, my soul, my all.[8]

Nor was he alone. The name of Charles Wesley (1707-1788)
is virtually synonymous with hymn singing. It is staggering
to think that, according to one estimate, he wrote 8,989
hymns, and yet not one before he was genuinely converted
at the age of 37—although already an ordained Anglican
minister! But after his conversion experience on Whitsunday
in 1738, he wrote what is generally accepted to be his first

7   For a list of 518 of Watts' hymns, see the entry on the CyberHymnal site:
www.cyberhymnal.org/bio/w/a/t/watts_i.htm
8   I Watts, 'When I Survey the Wondrous Cross', 1707.

hymn, 'Where Shall My Wondering Soul Begin?' And he couldn't stop singing.

These were saints who loved God with their heart, soul, mind, and strength. Their minds were soaked in the deep doctrines of the faith, and these wonderful truths had penetrated deep into their hearts. Consequently, they were men with a passion for singing. They could not help but speak—and speak in both prose and poetry—of what they had seen and heard, read and experienced. They knew the power of the song, and its potency to move and change the lives of others with the same gospel that had gripped and changed their own.

But they had more than a passion for singing; they had a passion for the truth. Their hymns are rich in gospel truths. Charles Wesley's hymns allude to all but four of the books of the Bible, and he drew from many sermons, or homilies, for his content. Speaking of his brother's hymns, John Wesley wrote that in his lyrics he produced, "a distinct and full account of scriptural Christianity".[9]

The Wesleys' concern that their songs preach the truth is seen in these words of John Wesley in a preface to a collection of their hymns:

> ...(you) gentlemen have done my brother and me... the honour to reprint many of our hymns. Now they are perfectly welcome to do so, provided they print them just as they are. Therefore, I must beg of them these two favours: either to let them stand just as they are, to take things for better or worse,

9   J Wesley, 'Preface' to *A Collection of Hymns for the Use of the People called Methodists*, John Mason, London, 1779, p. 4.

or to add the true reading in the margin, or at the bottom of the page, that we may no longer be accountable either for the nonsense or for the doggerel of other men.[10]

In other words, don't mess with the lyrics! The Wesleys were concerned that there might be a watering down of the rich theological content of their songs.

This is our musical heritage: songwriters who loved Jesus, loved gospel truth and were committed to expressing that love in congregational song. This book is, in part, a call to remember and honour their legacy.

But let's be clear about what this book is *not*, and what it *is*.

What this book is not

This book is *not* a book about Christian music generally. That is a much broader and more complex topic that would require a far longer book. Our focus in the chapters that follow is primarily on congregational singing.

This book is *not* an in-depth study of the Bible's teaching on the subject of worship. We are deliberately focusing on one aspect of what some call our 'corporate worship'—and a very important one, in our view—congregational singing.

This book is *not* a 'how to' book on congregational singing, or song leading, or improving the quality of music in your church. We have included some points of practical application in the final chapter, and various principles will be spelled out along the way, but the book is *not* intended

10   ibid.

to be a comprehensive manual for church musicians.

This book is *not* a plea to sing a particular style of song. You'll find no attempt in these pages to make a case for either contemporary songs over traditional hymns or for the superiority of the old over the new. While we recognize our indebtedness to the past, and believe it would be a terrible loss if we jettisoned those hymnic treasures, we are passionate to see contemporary Christian songs being written and sung.

What it is

First and foremost this book *is* an exploration of what the Bible says about God's people singing together.[11] Whilst not an exhaustive treatment of everything it says about singing, we'll see the various roles some of the Bible's key songs play in the contexts in which they're found. We'll also look at the content of each song, discovering what it has to teach us about God and his saving work for his people. We'll learn why the song is such an important vehicle for glorifying God and communicating profound theological truths to others.

11   The reason for looking at the Bible is simple. The Bible is the only divinely inspired and finally authoritative book that the church—and, indeed, the world—has been given. As such it is God's saving gift to the lost: able to make us wise for salvation through faith in Jesus Christ (2 Tim 3:15). It is likewise his sanctifying gift to the found: able to instruct us so that we might know how to live in the world and conduct ourselves in the household of God (1 Tim 3:15). Not only is much of the Bible given to us in the form of poetry or song, it has much to say about music and singing. If our church gatherings and corporate singing are to be honouring to God and edifying to his people, then we must pay attention to all that Scripture has to teach us about the God-given powers of congregational song.

This book *is* a passionate plea to give singing its proper place in the life of the church. It is a summons to harness the God-given power and potential of congregational singing, in order to refocus and revive our gatherings, giving God the praise that is due to him and encouraging one another more and more as we see the Day approaching (Heb 10:25).

This book *is* a call for God's people to recapture the best of our musical heritage, to make use of the best of our contemporary resources and to reform and refine our attitudes and practices according to God's word. To that end, we'll make occasional comments about the kind of songs we should sing and how we should sing them. In short, our call is to sing songs of scriptural substance, and to sing them with passion, clarity and sincerity in faith, hope and love.

Finally, this book is a reminder that singing will be a vital part of our experience of the life of the world to come, so it's important that we begin to get it right during our weekly rehearsals now. For who knows how much longer it will be before that great and glorious day comes when our Lord Jesus Christ will return and we will join with the myriads of angels, singing and praising our Creator and Redeemer, saying:

> "Salvation belongs to our God, who sits on the throne, and to the Lamb!... Amen! Blessing and glory and wisdom and thanksgiving and honour and power and might be to our God forever and ever! Amen." (Rev 7:10, 12)

Songs of the Saints

How to read this book

There are two ways to read our book, depending on whether you're a wader or a dipper.

Mike is a wader. He likes to begin at the beginning and wade through a book, chapter by chapter until the end. So if you decide to wade you'll be taken through the First Movement (looking at some of the songs of the Old Testament) to the Second Movement (looking at singing in the New Testament) before coming to the Third Movement and Finale (which look at the important issues surrounding congregational singing today).

Rob is more of a dipper, dipping here and there depending on his particular areas of interest. So, if you're also a dipper you might like to sing along with the first couple of chapters of the First Movement, and then perhaps another from the Second Movement, before skipping forward to the final three chapters that draw our thoughts together. You could then return later on to learn from some of the other songs of the Bible covered in the chapters you've skipped.

Whichever approach you choose, the audience has taken their seats. The instruments are tuned. The choir is ready. The conductor has tapped his baton. Let the songs begin.

The First Movement

2

The song of the warrior God (Exodus 15)

Let us remember that the very power of singing was given to human nature chiefly for this purpose, that our own warmest affections of soul might break out into natural or divine melody, and that the tongue of the worshipper might express his own heart.[12]

Isaac Watts

The hymn we love to hate

When Mike was a boy he sang hymns in school. Not a church school or a Christian school, but a government school. He attended regular chapel services, prayed and sang hymns. And, of course, he can still remember many of these hymns: 'The King of Love My Shepherd Is', 'Praise, My Soul, the King of Heaven', and one of our favourites (it was a boys' school after all), 'Onward, Christian Soldiers,

---

12   I Watts, *Psalms, Hymns and Spiritual Songs*, Thomas Ward & Co., London, 1839, p. 7.

marching as to war, with the cross of Jesus going on before'.[13]

Interestingly, we don't sing 'Onward, Christian Soldiers' much any more. We're not allowed to. It's been unceremoniously dumped from many hymnbooks. It was there in the old *Book of Common Praise*, but in 1977 when the Australian church published *The Australian Hymn Book*, it had fallen into such disfavour that the editors simply deleted it from the list.

And it wasn't just the Australian church that deleted it either. The Presbyterian Church of the USA has left it out for three hymnbooks now. This wasn't a response to some general neglect; indeed it led to a huge outcry from many ordinary pew sitters, who wanted their hymn back. But no such luck! However, when the editorial committees of the *Episcopal Hymn Book* and the *United Methodist Hymn Book* did the same thing, they came under so much popular pressure they eventually backed down and put it back in.

It seems that many hymnbook committees decided that singing this hymn was bad for us. Perhaps typical of such an attitude is Thomas Long, a Presbyterian professor of theology at Emory University, who in 2012 wrote:

> Good riddance. This hymn, with its 'hut-two-three-four' tune and its warring call for Christians to raise the battle flag, has long outlived its usefulness. Recently, one of my friends threatened to resign her role as church school assistant because the lead teacher insisted on having the children sing [it]. I stand with my friend.[14]

13   S Baring-Gould, 'Onward Christian Soldiers', 1865.
14   TG Long, 'The absurd in worship', *The Christian Century*, 13 August 2012 (viewed 14 September 2016): www.christiancentury.org/article/2012-08/absurd-worship

What a turnaround in one generation: from much-loved hymn to a reason for resigning a ministry!

Although still generally against using it, curiously Professor Long was caught off guard by this hymn in a way that surprised him. Each year when spending time at their summer house, he and his wife attend a small Methodist church in rural Maryland. There they worship amongst about 20 frail, elderly Christians, their numbers declining each year. One Sunday he turned up to see that the opening hymn was 'Onward, Christian Soldiers'. He groaned...

> But then we sang it, all twenty of us. The irony of the moment caught me off guard. There we were, most of us greying, some infirm, a hearing aid or two whistling in the background, singing, "Like a mighty army moves the church of God". If it hadn't been worship, I might have laughed out loud. Instead I teared up... There was a gospel truth here. Only in a place like this—a place where 'Onward, Christian Soldiers' was not a display of militarism but just patently ridiculous—could that hymn speak truth.[15]

How could Professor Long have missed the point for so long? The hymn was never a display of militarism. The opening line is, "marching *as* to war", not "marching *on* to war". It's a metaphor, and a common biblical metaphor for the believer's *spiritual* struggle, in which God displays his power in our weakness. "Join with me in suffering, like a good soldier of Christ Jesus" wrote Paul (2 Tim 2:3, NIV). He did not say *share in aggression* like a soldier. But *share in suffering* like a

15   ibid.

soldier. And it's *like* a soldier. And a soldier of *Jesus Christ*, who advanced his kingdom by being hung on a cross.

When the Reverend Sabine Baring-Gould wrote this hymn he needed something at the last minute for a Sunday School pageant. The song was hastily dashed off in 15 minutes to be sung by children who, as they sang of themselves as "a mighty army of God", must have looked as beautifully absurd as Professor Long's Maryland Methodists. It was never intended to be any more than a Sunday School song but, in today's terms, it 'went viral'. Arthur Sullivan wrote a tune and the rest, as they say, is history.

Sadly, the world never grasped the metaphor. In 1941, Winston Churchill and Franklin Roosevelt met on the battleship HMS Prince of Wales to agree to The Atlantic Charter. A church service was held, and Churchill was asked to choose the hymns. He chose 'Onward, Christian Soldiers'. In a radio broadcast afterwards he explained why:

> We sang 'Onward, Christian Soldiers' indeed, and I felt that this was no vain presumption, but that we had the right to feel that we were serving a cause for the sake of which a trumpet has sounded from on high.
>
> When I looked upon that densely packed congregation of fighting men of the same language, of the same faith, of the same fundamental laws and the same ideals... it swept across me that here was the only hope, but also the sure hope, of saving the world from measureless degradation.[16]

16 W Churchill, 'The Atlantic Charter', broadcast, London, 24 August 1941; reprinted in *Never Give In! Winston Churchill's Speeches*, Bloomsbury Academic, London, 2013, p. 252.

The allied armies the only hope of saving the world? Vain and blasphemous! What a far cry from the claim of the great hymn itself:

> Crowns and thrones may perish, kingdoms rise and
>   wane,
> But the Church of Jesus constant will remain.
> Gates of hell can never 'gainst that Church prevail;
> We have Christ's own promise, and that cannot fail.

Despite great armies, nations will rise and fall, but the only hope for people's salvation is Jesus Christ who, having disarmed the powers and authorities, made a public spectacle of them, triumphing over them by the cross (Col 2:15).[17]

God, and God alone, wins the salvation of his people. He did it once and for all on the cross by the death of his Son, an event he foreshadowed in Israel's great day of deliverance by the waters of the Red Sea. A salvation recounted in prose (in Exodus 14) and celebrated in song (in Exodus 15).

The battle is the Lord's: Exodus 14

The famous story of God saving his people out of the hands of the Egyptians is recorded in one of the most overtly God-centred passages in the Bible. The entire account deliberately highlights the activity of God and the passivity of man.

17   We are indebted to Rev. Matt Williams for these insights into 'Onward, Christian Soldiers'.

First, as they leave Egypt, God leads the Israelites into a cul-de-sac; he deliberately places them in a situation where they'll be hemmed in, with the advancing Egyptians on one side, and the sea behind them (vv. 1-2). Then verse 3 tells us God's purpose in making his people sitting ducks: "Pharaoh will say... 'the wilderness has shut them in'." God knows exactly how this fickle Egyptian king will respond, because he will harden Pharaoh's heart (v. 4). God will move Pharaoh so that, duped by God's strategy, he will bring his army out of Egypt and chase the Israelites to the shores of the Red Sea. God will move Pharaoh's heart so that God can triumph over him. And God will do that so that he will "get glory over Pharaoh and all his host, and the Egyptians shall know that I am the LORD" (v. 4).

Then we have a God-centred description of the defeat of the Egyptian army:

» the Lord drove the sea back (v. 21)
» the Lord threw the Egyptian army into a panic (v. 24)
» the Lord clogged their chariot wheels so that they drove heavily (v. 25)
» the Egyptians decide that with this God against them the battle is a lost cause and they cry out, "Let us flee from before Israel, for the LORD fights for them against the Egyptians" (v. 25)
» the Lord threw the Egyptians into the midst of the sea (v. 27)
» that day the Lord saved Israel from the hand of the Egyptians (v. 30).

And what was the result of it all? Israel saw God's great power against the Egyptians, so the people feared the Lord and they believed in the Lord, and in Moses his servant (v. 31).

And they sang.

The song of Moses: Exodus 15

Exodus 14 is a thoroughly God-centred account of an historical event. The chapter clearly affirms that the chief purpose of all that God does in this world is so that his name might be glorified. God deliberately, actively, sovereignly orders events to maximize the revelation of his glory. He hardens hearts, he changes minds, and he clogs wheels. Pharoahs, Nebuchadnezzars, Pilates, and Herods become tools in his hand so that God's name might be exalted, and the whole world might know that he is the Lord.

It is these great truths that ring out in the song of Moses and Miriam that we find recorded in Exodus 15. There is the much longer song of Moses, sung by Moses and the Israelites (vv. 1-18). And then Moses' sister leads the women of Israel in the much briefer chorus (v. 21).

Saved people sing

As we've seen in the lives of men like Watts and Wesley, when the Saviour God has captured someone's heart, forgiven their sins and worked in them the new birth, one of the spontaneous responses of the newly redeemed is to sing. They realize that God has done something incredible for them, something they could never have done for themselves. And he has done this both for his glory and as an expression of his grace. The only appropriate human response to this is wonder, praise and gratitude; a response that naturally finds its voice in singing.

This is precisely what we see taking place in the song of Moses. *When* the people of Israel experienced the saving grace of their God (14:21), *then* they couldn't help but burst into a song of praise to the Lord (15:1). In fact, this is a sequence we see repeatedly throughout Scripture: when God acts to save his people, his people are filled with joy, and when his people are filled with joy, they sing songs of praise to the Lord (see, for example, Pss 13:6, 98:1-6; Isa 12:1-6; Jas 5:13; Rev 5:9-10). But Exodus 15 is the first, and indeed paradigmatic, example of this marvellous sequence.

A word about the word 'praise'

In a book about the singing of God's people, it should be no surprise to encounter the word 'praise'. In fact, we're going to use it over 200 times (as do most translations of the Bible). But *what* does it mean and *how* are we using it? There is a wide range of Hebrew (Old Testament) and Greek (New Testament) words that can be (and often are) translated by our English word 'praise'. The essential idea that carries through them all is this: *to praise is to express respect, adoration or gratitude by declaring the greatness, goodness or worthiness of the object of our praise.* Whilst human beings can praise one another, our concern, in this book, is with the praise of God. In the Bible, such praise stems from the heart, is always verbalized, is often accompanied by music, dancing, clapping, and other bodily movements and usually has the effect of increasing God's fame. Whilst praise does not always have to take the form of singing, singing (as we've just seen) is a very natural, and often commanded, way of praising. We can also distinguish various aspects of praise: for example, shouts of praise, invitations to praise, promises to praise and, mostly importantly, articulations of the reasons for praise or expositions of God's worthiness to be praised. Finally, it's also important to note that God can be praised either directly (in words of adoration) or indirectly (in words of proclamation). In other words, both singing *to* God and singing *about* God are acts of praise.

The horse and his rider

Moses' song celebrates two great events: one in the recent past (vv. 10-12), and one in the near future (vv. 13-18). The redeemed singers look back and celebrate the salvation that has been won for them, and then they rejoice as they think to the future and the whole purpose of God's great saving work.

In various ways, the first half of the song celebrates how "the horse and rider he has thrown into the sea" (v. 1). In verses 1-5, Moses praises God for being the warrior God who saves him, and then summarizes all that God accomplished to set his people free: he hurled the army of Pharaoh into the sea; they were drowned; and the waters covered over them as they sank to the depths (vv. 4-5). Three slightly different aspects of the one great event.

In verses 6-8, Moses continues talking to God as he praises his power and majesty. God has a powerful right hand (v. 6). The blast of his nostrils, like those of a terrifying warhorse, split the waters, as they made ready to overwhelm their hapless victims.

In an almost mocking way, verses 9-10 rehearse the vain and foolish boastings of the ancient world's greatest, and most feared, army. But it took no more than a blowing of the divine breath and these same waters sent the army tumbling into its watery grave.

Finally, the choir sings its praises to this incomparably great God (v. 11), again rooting this worship in his great act of salvation.

Brilliantly, Moses has interwoven reminders of *how* Israel was saved with glorious affirmations of *who* has saved them. And the best Christian songs do that. The modern classic 'How Deep the Father's Love For Us', by Stuart Townend, does that. The song rehearses different aspects of Christ's atoning death for us. In the second stanza we're reminded of Christ's cry from the cross, "My God, my God, why have you forsaken me?" (Matt 27:46), as Townend writes, "The Father turns his face away". The next stanza reminds us, as the four Gospels do, of the mockery Christ faced as he hung on the cross. The final stanza celebrates that by this death everything that needed to be done for our salvation was accomplished: "I know that it is finished". And the song's triumphant final line reminds us that his death has paid our ransom. Different vignettes of the cross all interwoven in a hymn of praise: divine abandonment; scorned by people; finished work; ransom paid.

And interspersed throughout this modern hymn, there is praise to God. The depth of his love is beyond estimation. At great personal cost he gave his only Son. Our only boast can be in what Jesus has done for us in his death and resurrection.

Mike was in a church recently where they sang for about 20 minutes, but none of the songs spoke of the gospel. At no point was the congregation reminded of *what* God had done for them. Such times of singing fall far short of what the Saviour God delights in. Remember, while Moses and Miriam penned the words of Exodus 15, "all Scripture is breathed out by God" (2 Tim 3:16) and "whatever was written in former days was written for our instruction" (Rom 15:4). That's why so much of this book is describing singing *in the Bible*. Since God inspired these songs, then these songs can be relied upon to teach and guide us about how God himself wants us to sing to him. Just as reading the prayers of the Bible teaches us to pray, so the songs of the saints of Scripture teach us to sing. For example, it's often striking how different the prayers of the apostle Paul are from our own and, similarly, there are some striking differences between the Bible's songs and some contemporary songs.

Guide us, o thou great Jehovah

In the second half of the song of Moses (vv. 13-18), the great leader reminds Israel of the purpose of her salvation. God has saved them out of Egypt to bring them to his "holy abode". They've been saved by God's power to live in God's presence.

In this half of the song, verses 13 and 17 serve as bookends, reminding Israel that their salvation is an act of covenant love. They are the Good Shepherd's sheep and he is guiding them to his home (v. 13). They are the fruit he will plant in his dwelling place, where they can prosper and flourish (v. 17). These images speak of God's loving choice of Israel, his promise to guide and lead them, and their hope that, ultimately, they will dwell in the sanctuary of the Lord.

Sandwiched between these glorious and comforting pictures of God's presence with his people, Moses forecasts the terror that will come upon the surrounding nations when they hear of God's mighty wonders at the Red Sea (vv. 15-16). What a contrast to the arrogant boastings of the Egyptians (v. 9). In the days to come, these pagan nations will hear and tremble (v. 14); there will be "terror and dread", and they'll be as "still as a stone" (v. 16). The picture is of the nations, paralysed by fear, and holding their collective breaths, while this nation led by the awesome warrior God walks on by.

The songs God wants us to sing celebrate *both* what he has done, and his eternal purposes in winning salvation for us. Our Christian songs must turn our eyes backwards and forwards. Our songs must regularly take us back to the cross, celebrating the glory, power, grace and majesty of our warrior God.

And it is so important that our songs lift our eyes beyond the here and now, which so consumes our thoughts, anxieties, dreams and prayers, to the place where God is leading us. William Williams' classic hymn, 'Guide me, O Thou Great Jehovah', does this for us:

> When I tread the verge of Jordan, bid my anxious
>   fears subside;
> bear me through the swelling current, land me safe
>   on Canaan's side;
> Songs of praises, songs of praises, I will ever give
>   to thee.[18]

18   W Williams, 'Guide me, O Thou Great Jehovah', 1745.

The importance of Exodus 15

On a number of levels, the song of Moses is a biblical classic. It's important in the book of Exodus, as it marks a turning point in the narrative. The first 14 chapters describe the events leading up to God's great saving work at the Red Sea. From chapter 16 onwards Israel begins her journey to Sinai. The songs of Exodus 15 are the bridge between the two halves of the book.

But Exodus 15 is also important because, as we've seen, it's paradigmatic for other songs that God's saved people will sing. We'll look shortly at the songs of Deborah and Hannah, and both of them will rejoice in the warrior God. In the days of the Judges, Deborah rejoices in the Lord's victory over the people of Edom (Judg 5:4). Later Hannah will celebrate that "the bows of the mighty are broken" by the Lord (1 Sam 2:4).

But the song of Moses also catapults us to the end of the Bible, and the victory songs of Revelation. In particular, John sees and hears another great crowd beside a sea (Rev 15:1-8). Like the redeemed by the Red Sea, this group also rejoices in the great victory God has won for them. And John tells us that "They held harps given them by God and sang the song of God's servant Moses *and of the Lamb*" (vv. 2b-3, NIV). For the salvation of God's people is now complete. The true Moses, the Lord Jesus, has come and destroyed our ultimate enemy, Satan, who had enslaved God's people. By his own death, God's first-born has brought his people out from the true slavery, to sin and death, by the last and great exodus. As the nations before the first exodus trembled, so the hope of this song is that all the nations will turn and worship:

"Great and amazing are your deeds,
    O Lord God the Almighty!
Just and true are your ways,
    O King of the nations!
Who will not fear, O Lord,
    and glorify your name?
For you alone are holy.
    All nations will come
    and worship you,
for your righteous acts have been revealed."
        (Rev 15:3-4)

The battle belongs to the Lord

It is good to sing songs that praise the Lord, our victorious warrior. And it is important to sing songs which remind Christians that while the Great Battle has been fought and won by Christ on the cross, we still "wrestle against... rulers and authorities", wearing the armour of God (Eph 6:11-12), and we fight "the good fight" (2 Tim 4:7). It is wise to give the exhortation, 'Onward, Christian Soldiers'. Indeed, there is so much truth and encouragement in these words:

At the sign of triumph Satan's host doth flee;
On then, Christian soldiers, on to victory.
Hell's foundations quiver at the shout of praise;
Brothers, lift your voices, loud your anthems raise.

Such stirring words remind us of Christ's triumph over the hosts of darkness, and give to the contemporary church a much-needed exhortation not to fear the one

Songs of the Saints

who has been robbed of his malevolent power.

And then the marvellous third verse reminds us that, despite our diversity as God's people, there is much more that unites us than divides us:

Like a mighty army moves the Church of God;
Brothers, we are treading where the Saints have trod.
We are not divided, all one body we,
One in hope and doctrine, one in charity.

One of the most disturbing trends in the contemporary church is the growth of biblical illiteracy. Increasingly, people do not seem to know, or even care very much about, the great truths of the faith. And basic Bible knowledge is sadly lacking. Undoubtedly, there are a number of reasons for this spreading theological ignorance, but the songs we sing are partly to blame. The songs we sing shape the truths we believe. It's so important for Christian faith and maturity that as Christian people we know our past. We need to know, understand, and continually remind ourselves of what Jesus has done for us. And we must know our future. We are a pilgrim people, travelling through this barren land, but heading for our heavenly home, "the place, O LORD, which you have made for your abode, the sanctuary, O Lord, which your hands have established" (Exod 15:17). The songs we sing remind us of our purpose and our destiny, and inspire and encourage us to keep moving forward.

Theology and music. Truth and singing. They belong together, and what God has joined together we should never separate.

3

A song of triumph and trust (Judges 5)

The Lion was pacing to and fro about that empty land and singing his new song. It was softer and more lilting than the song by which he had called up the star and the sun; a gentle, rippling music. And as he walked and sang the valley grew green with grass. It spread out from the Lion like a pool. It ran up the sides of the little hills like a wave.[19]

CS Lewis

Silly love songs

"Some people say the world has had enough of silly love songs."[20]

Judging by the popularity of 'pop music' radio stations, and judging by what tops the music charts, the world will

---

19   CS Lewis, *The Magician's Nephew*, HarperCollins, London, 1995, p. 97.
20   P McCartney, 'Silly Love Songs', 1976.

never have its fill of silly love songs. Paul McCartney was surely right! And, to be perfectly candid, we aren't complaining. We love pop music. In fact, Rob doesn't just love it—he still writes and performs it!

Mind you, the fact that we are pop music aficionados doesn't mean we are blind to the reality that much of what passes for music today is banal, mindless and vacuous. There are, of course, some songs of substance to be found out there in radio-land, but they are rarely heard amidst the din of the many mushy, gushy, silly love songs.

Songs of substance stand out because they have the power to do far more than entertain. They can challenge and inspire. They can stimulate thought and action. And as we saw with the songs of the slaves, there are even a few, a select coterie, that are so powerful that sometimes they change a society.

One such song is a lament immortalized by the great blues singer Billie Holiday. It's called 'Strange Fruit', and it paints a graphic picture of the lynching of a black man:

Southern trees bear strange fruit,
Blood on the leaves and blood at the root,
Black bodies swinging in the southern breeze,
Strange fruit hanging from the poplar trees.

Pastoral scene of the gallant south,
The bulging eyes and the twisted mouth,
Scent of magnolias, sweet and fresh,
Then the sudden smell of burning flesh.

Here is fruit for the crows to pluck,
For the rain to gather, for the wind to suck,

For the sun to rot, for the trees to drop,
Here is a strange and bitter crop.[21]

The song was written in 1938 by Abel Meerapol; a Jewish schoolteacher from the Bronx in New York. Meerapol was inspired to put his emotions into song when he saw a photo of the lynching of two black men. Not surprisingly, Billie Holiday's record label refused to record such a controversial song. Undeterred she went and recorded it on a specialty label instead. It quickly became the anthem for the anti-lynching movement. It's been said that the powerful lyrics and melody made it impossible for white Americans and politicians to continue to ignore the Southern campaign of racist terror.[22]

It's a striking tale! In the mid-20th century, in the racist South of the United States of America, a man and woman write and sing a song that not only expresses the anger of a nation, but helps change a society.

But they were not the first. Over 3000 years earlier another man and woman wrote and sang a song, and this song, too, caught up and expressed all the fears and hopes of an oppressed people. It too ushered in generational change. The woman's name was Deborah, the wife of Lappidoth. The man's name was Barak, the son of Abinoam. Their song is found in Judges chapter 5.

21   A Meerapol, 'Strange Fruit', 1938.
22   M Washington, 'We've Come This Far By Faith', blog posted 21 January 2013 (viewed 5 August 2016): www.sistassavingsistasforchrist.com/blog/2013/01/21/Strange-Fruit-Weve-Come-This-Far-By-Faith-Happy-Birthday-Martin.aspx

The battle that birthed the song

No songs of substance are written in a historical vacuum and every song has a story. Just as Abel Meerapol saw a photograph of two men lynched by whites and expressed his horror in the words of a song, so too, after years of oppression, wretchedness, and despair, a glorious Israelite victory gives birth to a song of trust and triumph.

The story begins in Judges 4 where we read that, yet again, Israel has sinned against the Lord (v. 1), presumably by returning to their old ways and giving themselves over to idolatry (cf. 2:11-13, 3:7). As an act of discipline, the Lord handed the people over to a king called Jabin, one of the pagan kings of Canaan (v. 2). However, the focus of attention in the story is on the commander of his army, Sisera. For more than 20 years this deadly duo had oppressed Israel, and the text tells us the secret of Sisera's military strength: "he had 900 chariots of iron" (v. 3).

On the other side is a somewhat unlikely pair. Verse 4 tells us that judging Israel at the time was a woman called Deborah. Her name means, literally, 'honey bee', which, as we will see, is quite appropriate since a bee is famous not only for its honey but also its sting. And, for some, the sting of the bee is fatal! But Deborah is more than just a judge; she is a prophetess and, as such, she announces from the Lord that he will give victory to Israel in the ensuing battle (v. 7). At Deborah's side is the somewhat timid general, named Barak. It is his duty to rally the troops and lead them into battle.

The writer then briefly describes the battle, and the defeat of the Canaanite army (vv. 12-16). The climax of the story is the graphic description of the ignominious end of Sisera, who is rather humiliatingly killed by a woman armed only with a hammer and a tent peg (vv. 17-22). The battle-weary enemy king flees to the tent of a woman called Jael (whom he believed to be an ally). She invites the unsuspecting Sisera to enter her tent so he can hide and be refreshed. If Deborah is the honeybee, then Jael is the spider and the fly has just flown into her web!

After being lulled to sleep by Jael's hospitality of drink and rest, our unlikely hero quietly sneaks up beside him and places a large tent peg on the side of his head. With one powerful swing, Jael drives the thick peg through his temple "until it went down into the ground" (v. 21). At that point, the text (rather unnecessarily) informs us, "he died".

In the song that follows in the next chapter, Deborah and Barak slowly, and with deliberate repetition, drive home his demise:

> "Between her feet
>   he sank, he fell, he lay still;
> between her feet
>   he sank, he fell;
> where he sank,
>   there he fell—dead." (Judg 5:27)

Chapter 4 ends by telling us of the subsequent destruction of Jabin, and the completeness of the victory won that day over the enemies of God and his people (vv. 23-24). No wonder Deborah and Barak will later conclude their song by singing:

> "So may all your enemies perish, O LORD!
>   But your friends be like the sun as he rises in his
>   might." (Judg 5:31)

The ballad of Deborah and Barak

After the destruction of their oppressors, the leaders of Israel break into song. For the benefit of future generations, the biblical historian records the duet that Deborah and Barak sang and, presumably, wrote together. This ancient 'She & Him' now retell the story of the battle, and in so doing give us some additional information about it that the narrative in chapter 4 hadn't included.

But we need to remember that it is a song. It is, therefore, not only intended to inform, but to thrill and exhilarate, to stir up joy, wonder and thanksgiving to the glory of God. So whilst it clearly seeks to educate the mind and quicken the memory by rehearsing all that God has accomplished for Israel, the purpose of such education is to engage the whole person—mind, heart and will—in exultant praise at the triumphs of the Lord. Consequently, it is a song of both profound theological depth and enormous emotional power.

Being poetry, the song is divided into various stanzas, each one recounting the positive contribution, or otherwise, of the tribes of Israel to the battle against Jabin. But its main focus and subject is God. He is the true victor. From the outset it is clear that this is the real source of the song's emotional energy. "Bless the LORD!" command Deborah and Barak in verse 2. "To the LORD I will sing; I will make melody to the LORD, the God of Israel", they go on to say (v. 3).

So often, inarticulate sports stars confess that their glorious Grand Final victory leaves them lost for words. When asked how they feel, in the midst of a cacophony of clichés (e.g. "It's a dream come true"), they confess that the whole experience is indescribable. They admit they can't put into words their emotions of exultation and relief. Well, that wasn't a problem for Deborah and Barak. There was nothing indescribable about how they felt. For 31 song-filled magnificent verses they explicitly put into words exactly what happened and how they now feel.

The song begins by praising the leaders of the tribes of Israel for willingly offering themselves to the Lord's service to fight against his enemies (5:2). When the rulers of Israel finally decide to match their confession that the Lord is God with action, expressed in taking up weapons against the Canaanites, then the enemies of God should tremble. So, watch out kings of Canaan for Israel is on the move.

But, as we've already noted, it is actually the Lord who is on the move. And when the God of Israel rouses himself to save his people then "the earth trembled" (v. 4). Indeed, it may well have been literally the case that, "the heavens dropped, yes, the clouds dropped water" (v. 4). For later, Deborah will recall how "the torrent Kishon swept them away" (v. 21). It is quite possible that this is how Israel actually defeated Sisera and why their chariots, which had previously given them the upper hand in battle, proved so useless on this occasion. The Lord had sent a flash flood that meant their wheels got stuck in the mud. Suddenly there was an even playing field; fighter against fighter.

The ballad, then, turns into something of a dirge as Deborah and Barak sadly recount what life was like in Canaan under the tyranny of Jabin. The roads were abandoned because the people were scared to travel openly. Instead, they either took to the side paths or stayed at home (vv. 6-7). However, sorrow turns to hopeful pride as

Deborah and Barak again praise the Lord for the princes of Israel who joined the common people and gathered for battle. When Deborah gave her summons to war, men came from Ephraim, Benjamin, and Zebulun (vv. 9-14).

But it wasn't all good news; support was not unanimous. While some joined Deborah and Barak and followed them into battle, others sat back and did nothing. When the time came to fight and throw off the oppressor, tribes like Reuben, Asher and Dan, even after some soul searching, decided to stay by their sheep pens, listen to the songs of the shepherds, and stay where they were (vv. 15-16).

When we turn to the next stanza (vv. 19-23) one immediately feels the rise in emotional intensity as the battle is described. Images pile on top of each other. Even heaven and earth seemed to mirror the events on the battlefield, as the stars of heaven were locked in mortal combat (v. 20), and the river swept away the vanquished (v. 21). "March on, my soul, with might," the people sang. Indeed, the thundering of the horses' hooves in the next line seems to echo the thunderous voices of the confident army of the Lord as they march toward victory (v. 22).

The mood of the song continually changes. From a word of curse to the town of Meroz for not joining with the people of God (v. 23), Deborah then praises the brave exploits of Jael and her tent peg (vv. 24-27). One can imagine the trumpets, horns and cymbals being silenced as flutes and harps accompany the celebration of this brave demonstration of faith.

However, this remarkable poem doesn't end there. Finally, and brilliantly, Deborah and Barak portray the pathos of the defeat of Sisera by focusing on his waiting mother (vv. 28-30). This is powerful poetry. There she stands, waiting by the window, wondering why her beloved son is taking so long to return. He should have been home by now. How many times have a million anxious mothers, waiting for their sons to come home, echoed those words? The minutes tick by. Tears begin to fill her eyes. Of course, there is probably a perfectly reasonable explanation, or so her ladies-in-waiting tell her. He's late because there is so much booty to collect and bring back. There are colourful garments, highly embroidered for her neck. And, of course, two women for every man!

One of the most tragic 'spoils of war' is the women—the mothers, the sisters, the daughters—whom victorious armies have all too often raped and abused. Literally, the Hebrew says, "a womb, a pair of wombs" for each man. That's all the vanquished women have become: wombs. Hardly even human beings. Just objects for sexual pleasure and plunder. Bodies to be used and abused. It's vulgar and crude, and it seems even more despicable on the lips of another woman. Doesn't she have daughters? Sisters? So, any sympathy we have for her is mitigated by the fact that she can condone, and even celebrate, her son's treatment of conquered women as plunder to be enjoyed. She waits, but we who sing this song already know what she will only discover with certainty later: her son has been felled by the hand of a woman (5:27)!

And so the song comes to an end. The enemies of Israel have been subdued. God has, once again, delivered his people. The next generation are the beneficiaries, for as the final words of the chapter tell us: "the land had rest for forty years" (5:31).

Learning from the song of Deborah

How can you make your church grow? What is the 'secret of success' of those churches whose numbers have exploded? Most experts today would agree that, whatever else you do, you must get the music right. One thing most successful churches share in common is a commitment to a high-quality music ministry. And that means singing songs that people like to sing and making them sound the way that people like to hear them. That means listening to the kind of music popular on the local radio stations. And today that means soft rock. It is the kind of music that's light on the ears and, often, light on the brain. It's light and easy. So, today, wherever you travel from Melbourne to Mongolia, or from New York to Nairobi, you'll find in most churches the same kind of music, the same songs, the same style, with the same kind of 'worship team'. It's the McDonaldization of worship. Tasty, perhaps—but of questionable nutritional value.

Of course, the danger is that if you select music that is 'light and easy' on the ears, it will be difficult to convey those truths that are hard to hear, confronting to the conscience or challenging to the will. Theory and practice need to go together. There must be a congruity between the music we select or compose and the truths we wish to convey through this music.

While the music that accompanied the song of Deborah and Barak has been lost to us, we can still learn much from the content of this paean of praise. One of the most striking lessons of this remarkable song is how it relates, in considerable detail, the triumphs of the God who works salvation for his people and brings a just judgement on his (and their) enemies. The first verse calls on the people to praise the Lord for the victory he has won. This sets the agenda for the rest of the song. While the ballad describes the various contributions of the participants in the battle (and the culpability of the abstainers) implicitly all that has been accomplished is the work of the Lord.

Again and again, the songs of Scripture don't just invite us to praise the Lord, but give us a mountain of reasons why we should do so.

Of course, there is a time and place simply to 'sing hallelujah to the Lord' or, like Psalm 150 does, to call others to do so. But typically Scripture tells us what the Lord has done that makes him so worthy of praise, and arguably Psalm 150 presupposes that we've digested the content of Psalms 1-149! That's why Tony Payne is on to something when he colourfully compares songs of praise to advertising.[23] An advertisement proclaims the virtues of the product with the intention that people, having seen its merits, will sacrifice what they have to possess it. So, the song of praise, like the advertising jingle, describes and promotes the glories of God, declares and celebrates his wonderful deeds, so that people might have ample reasons to take hold of this salvation. Oh that more of our contemporary praise anthems gave such reasons!

Majesty, worship His Majesty. *Why?*
Unto Jesus, be all glory, honour and praise! *Why?*
Majesty, Kingdom authority,

---

23 T Payne, 'Confessions of a teenage praise junkie', *The Briefing*, 20 February 1996 (viewed 5 August 2016): www.matthiasmedia.com/briefing/1996/02/confessions-of-a-teenage-praise-junkie

Flow from His throne, unto His own
His anthem raise. *OK. But please tell me more!*

So exalt, lift up on High the name of Jesus. *Sure,*
        but why?
Magnify, come glorify Christ Jesus, the King! *Please*
        tell me why.
Majesty, worship His Majesty. *For heaven's sake, tell*
        me why!
Jesus, who died, now glorified,
King of all Kings! *Ah, now you're beginning to tell*
        me why![24]

Why pick on Jack Hayford's much loved, Christian classic, 'Majesty' (that has encouraged many) to make our point? Because, frankly, it's 'light on' at the level of reasons to praise. It rightly and persistently invites us to glorify and magnify the Lord Jesus Christ, but only in the final line, and then only briefly, reminds us why.

Now, admittedly, not every song has to do every job. But the songs that are of most help to God's people, and consequently are often the most enduring, contain both *strong exhortations* to praise as well as *substantial reasons* for praise. 'Majesty' is strong on the first and weak on the second. But at least it gets to the second. Sadly, there are far too many contemporary songs that don't get there at all. The world may never have had enough of silly love songs, but the church of Jesus Christ could certainly do with less silly praise songs!

24   J Hayford, 'Majesty', 1981.

The songs of the book of Revelation, some of which we will look at in more detail later, are not only full of praise to God but also full of *reasons*. For example:

"Worthy are you, our Lord and God,
    to receive glory and honour and power,
for you created all things..." (4:11)

"Worthy are you to take the scroll
    and to open its seals,
*for you were slain, and by your blood you ransomed people
        for God
    from every tribe...*" (5:9)

"We give thanks to you, Lord God Almighty,
    who is and who was,
*for you have taken your great power
    and begun to reign.*" (11:17)

"Hallelujah!
Salvation and glory and power belong to our God,
    for his judgements are true and just..." (19:1-2)

"Hallelujah!
For our Lord God
    the Almighty reigns.
Let us rejoice and exult
    and give him the glory,
for the marriage of the Lamb has come..." (19:6b-7)

In light of these examples, the popular and simple little chorus by Tommy Walker comes much closer to the biblical pattern of praise:

He came to live, live a perfect life
He came to be the living word, our light
He came to die, so we'd be reconciled
He came to rise, to show his power and might and
That's why we praise him, that's why we sing...[25]

Conclusion

We have read in this often-neglected Old Testament book of Judges another of the Lord's mighty acts of salvation. Certainly he used Deborah and Barak and Jael to win his great victory, just like he has used people in your life to bring salvation to you. Yet, from beginning to end we have seen both described and celebrated the truth that salvation is God's work. All glory ultimately goes to him.

We need to learn to praise the Lord like Deborah and Barak. Deborah and Barak, who experienced and sang of God's amazing grace. Deborah and Barak, whose song tells us of the Father's deep love for us, who enumerate verse by verse his great faithfulness, and who remind us of his mercies, which are new morning by morning.

And if Israel had cause to sing God's praises by recalling his mighty acts, how much more we who are his new covenant people, we who have witnessed a salvation so great, so wonderful, so complete that no other battle need ever be fought again as we are now "saved from our enemies and from the hand of all who hate us" (Luke 1:71). In dying our death and rising again to new life, Christ has delivered us from our bondage to sin and

25   T Walker, 'That's Why We Praise Him', 1999.

has so triumphed over Satan's kingdom that "the powers of evil have received a blow from which they can never recover".[26]

More than that, God by his Spirit has put faith and repentance into our hearts, has given us new birth into a living hope, and has filled us with his Holy Spirit who empowers us to live for him in the present and long for his return in the future. Therefore, the most natural thing in all the world for people who have been so wonderfully and miraculously rescued is to declare and celebrate their deliverance in song. And so, we end this chapter taking the words of Judges 5:3 and marrying them with Colossians 1:13-14:

> To the LORD I will sing;
> I will make melody to the LORD, the God of Israel.
> He has delivered us from the domain of darkness
> and transferred us to the kingdom of his beloved
>   Son,
> in whom we have redemption, the forgiveness of
>   sins.

26   AM Hunter, *Interpreting Paul's Gospel*, SCM Press, London, 1954, p. 127.

4

When singers ruled the earth (1 and 2 Chronicles)

I always love music; who so has skill in this art, is of a good temperament, fitted for all things. We must teach music in schools; a schoolmaster ought to have skill in music, or I would not regard him. Neither should we ordain young men as preachers, unless they have been well exercised in music.[27]

Martin Luther

Let's just praise the Lord

What do we think we're doing when we sing together in church? Many would say, "We're praising the Lord, of course". That's right, but is that *all* we're doing?

In 1 Corinthians 14, in order to help the Corinthian Christians better understand why they come together as

---

27   M Luther, *The Table Talk of Martin Luther*, trans. and ed. William Hazlitt, HG Bohn, London, 1857, p. 340.

the church, the apostle Paul outlines some of the activities that mark their assemblies:

> When you come together, each of you has a hymn, or a word of instruction, a revelation, a tongue or an interpretation. Everything must be done so that the church may be built up. (1 Cor 14:26, NIV)

Notice what Paul does not say. He does not say, "When you come together to teach each other and build each other up (that is, through instruction, a revelation and a tongue), don't forget to also praise the Lord and have a time of worship (sing a hymn)". No, all the activities Paul mentions (hymn, word of instruction, revelation, tongue and interpretation) all serve the same purpose: the building up or strengthening of the church.

This might surprise us. Certainly, we would all see the word of instruction, the revelation and the interpreted tongue as various ways of bringing God's word to his people, but would we see the hymn in the same way? Yet here in this chapter at the head of Paul's list of word-based activities that build up the church, he places the song. Yes, in song we praise the Lord. Yes, in song, we give thanks to the Lord for he is good. But here—and elsewhere—Paul also sees singing as an important way of teaching and strengthening the congregation.

From where did Paul get this rather elevated view of the role of singing in the church? Not surprisingly, from his Bible. But, perhaps surprisingly, from 1 and 2 Chronicles—books which speak to us of a time in Israel's history when singers ruled the earth.

The flowering of Israelite singing

The spiritual, material and military high point of Israel's history were the reigns of David and Solomon. Both these men made grave mistakes and both sowed seeds that led, eventually, to the nation's schism and downfall. But for about 80 years, it looked, at least on the surface, like God's ancient promises made to Abraham (Gen 12:1-3) might be fulfilled. God's people, as numerous as the sand on the seashore, lived peacefully in a land of prosperity, with God dwelling in their midst in his temple in Jerusalem. This period was marked by victory on the battlefield, marvellous building programs, and a flowering of wisdom *and music*. Indeed one of the most striking features of this Golden Age in Israel's history was the prominence given to singing.

Again and again at the highpoints of Israel's spiritual life we find the people singing and celebrating the Lord. We see this particularly in these two often-neglected books of the Bible, 1 and 2 Chronicles.

This two-volume work is one of the two accounts the Bible gives us of the history of Israel from the rise of the monarchy—that is, Saul (1050-1010), David (1010-970), and Solomon (970-930)—to the fall of Jerusalem and Judah's exile in to Babylon in 587 BC. The other account is found in the books of Samuel and Kings. While there is considerable overlap between the books of Chronicles and these other books, Chronicles brings a unique perspective to Israel's history.

One of the chief purposes of the books of Chronicles is to highlight the way in which God relates to his people and his people are to relate to him. That's why the building of the temple in Jerusalem and the role of the Levitical priesthood are emphasized.

David, the ark and the singers

Pre-eminently, 1 Chronicles is the story of David, Israel's ideal king, but it's a selective biography. There's no defeat of Goliath, no adultery with Bathsheba, and no rebellion by Absalom. Instead, the two events which are of most interest to the biblical author are the bringing of the ark of the covenant into Jerusalem (chapters 13-16) and, most important of all, the preparations for the building of the temple—the sign that, at last, God is dwelling in the midst of his people (chapters 17, 22-29).

As they are about to carry the ark inside the city, the main focus of the narrative is on David's appointment of singers and musicians to lead the procession. The rest of the chapter (15:16-29) and also the next describe the people, including their king, as they commit themselves to "play loudly on musical instruments, on harps and lyres and cymbals, to raise sounds of joy" (v. 16). What is clear from this is that God's presence in the midst of his people is a supremely joyful event. In fact, in this instance, important as their other roles and duties are, the ministry of music before the ark in Jerusalem is central to the ministry of the Levitical priesthood.

Chapter 16 also records a psalm of thanksgiving that David commits to the choir leader, Asaph (who himself wrote a number of psalms), and the other ministers in music. Drawing from Psalms 105, 96 and 106 this song extols God as both creator and saviour, and, as Andrew

Hill points out, serves as the theological centre of the chronicler's retelling of Israel's history.[28] The coming of the ark of the covenant to Jerusalem and the building of the temple marked the pinnacle of Israel's life and hope. Central to her experience of *shalom* in the Promised Land was the presence of the living God in her midst. For the greatest joy and blessing that God's people can know is to be in the presence of God. This is what Adam and Eve enjoyed in the beginning, and what will be the defining feature of the age to come (Revelation 21-22). For a brief time, in symbolic anticipation of this ultimate future, God's people experienced that divine dwelling in the days of David and Solomon.

How, then, do God's people respond appropriately to the presence of the God who is now in their midst? One of the answers the chronicler gives is that "David also commanded the chiefs of the Levites to appoint their brothers as the singers who should play loudly on musical instruments, on harps and lyres and cymbals, to raise sounds of joy" (15:16). That's why Andrew Hill is right to describe the function of 1 and 2 Chronicles as "a call to celebration, praising God for who he is as the only true God, and thanking him for what he has done to restore the pre-Fall creation order and to redeem fallen humanity".[29]

28 AE Hill, *The NIV Application Commentary: 1 and 2 Chronicles*, Zondervan, Grand Rapids, 2003, p. 239.
29 ibid., p. 40.

David, the temple and the singers

The same emphasis is found in 1 Chronicles' lengthy account of David's preparations for the building of the temple later in the book (chapters 22-29). Much of the section comprises various lists of names of those involved in this work: the priests, the gatekeepers, the treasurers, the soldiers... and the singers. Chapter 25, in particular, describes the various musical guilds that were, presumably, rostered on to lead the worship in and around the temple.

But note two things of importance. First, it is King David and the commanders of the army who set apart the musicians (25:1). This association of music and warfare is something we will see again later in Chronicles.

Second, and strikingly, the singers and musicians are set apart "for the ministry of prophesying" (v. 1, NIV). Repeatedly, as the chronicler tables the names of the singers and musicians, he describes them as the ones "who prophesied with the lyre in thanksgiving and praise to the LORD" (v. 3). Singers as prophets! Singing as prophesying! Why does the chronicler describe their ministry in this way? First, because their praise and thanksgiving was understood to be the result of divine inspiration. This is stressed repeatedly in the books of Chronicles; the Lord himself both commanded and enabled this ministry (2 Chr 29:25).

Second, because of the vital teaching role their ministry played. This can be seen from an examination of the content of the 12 psalms ascribed to Asaph in the book of Psalms (Psalms 50, 73-83). These psalms speak of the believer's doubts and questions (Psalms 73, 74, 79), rehearse God's faithfulness, despite Israel's disobedience, throughout her history (Psalms 78, 81), and provide comfort by reminding God's people of the Lord who is their Saviour and Judge (Psalms 50, 75, 76, 80). In other words, in the act of worship, the 'singing prophets' both led the people in praise and edified them by addressing profound theological questions of life and faith, all the while reminding them of the character and deeds of their faithful, sovereign God.

It's not surprising, then, that the apostle Paul includes the hymn as part of the teaching ministry that takes place when God's people gather. Such an understanding also lies behind his instructions concerning singing in his letter to the Colossians: "Let the word of Christ dwell in you richly, teaching and admonishing one another in all wisdom, singing psalms and hymns and spiritual songs" (3:16). We see here the way in which Paul's thought-world resonates with that of the chronicler. Having Christ's word dwell in us is tantamount to the dwelling of God himself! As we've seen in Chronicles, when God dwells with his people this expresses itself in joyful praise and thanksgiving. But for both Paul and the author of Chronicles the songs we sing are one very important means by which we teach and admonish one another. But more of that in chapter 7.

Fighting with flutes!

Before we leave the world of Chronicles there is one more fascinating incident we need to look at which, again, emphasizes the important role that singers and songs played in the life of God's covenant people.

About 100 years after Solomon, a godly king by the

name of Jehoshaphat was on the throne. He is a relatively minor character in the book of 1 Kings, but the chronicler gives this righteous leader four whole chapters, because he is one of the model kings of Judah. Still, godliness does not provide an insurance policy against trouble, and it is a dark day for Judah. It is around 850 or 860 BC, and towards the end of Jehoshaphat's reign some of the neighbouring powers form an alliance against him. He is hopelessly outnumbered and, humanly speaking, the situation is impossible. It is in this context that we see the measure of the man.

The first thing the king does, quite appropriately, is pray. His prayer expresses his conviction that God's power can change any situation, even without human co-operation:

> In your hand are power and might, so that none is able to withstand you... For we are powerless against this great horde that is coming against us. We do not know what to do, but our eyes are on you. (2 Chr 20:6b, 12b).

The Lord hears the prayer of the king and (reminiscent of the days of Deborah) through a word of prophecy assures the people that they will be delivered (vv. 14-17). What's more, they won't have to lift a finger, for the Lord will fight the battle for them. In faith, the army then marches out to battle, but look who Jehoshaphat puts on the frontlines:

> ...[Jehoshaphat] appointed those who were to sing to the LORD and praise him in holy attire, as they went before the army... (v. 21)

The song they sing is one that any reader of Chronicles is now well familiar with. It is the song that was sung as David brought the ark into Jerusalem (1 Chr 16:34), and also as Solomon brought this same ark into the newly completed temple building (2 Chr 5:13). It is the simple but profound song of thanksgiving:

"Give thanks to the LORD,
    for his steadfast love endures forever." (v. 21b)

Back in 1 Chronicles 6 we read that King David appointed the Kohathites, from the tribe of Levi, to minister with music before the temple of the Lord. They had been doing that ever since. Now, as Judah marches into battle with the promise of certain victory, the people are led by this very same church choir (although, by now it would be their grandchildren and great grandchildren!). These men aren't soldiers, fighters or charioteers; they are singers, guitarists, trumpeters and song writers. It is these Levites who lead the armies of God's people:

And when they began to sing and praise, the LORD set an ambush against the men of Ammon, Moab and Mount Seir, who had come against Judah, so that they were routed (v. 22).

In the days when singers ruled the earth, we have this amazing story of the singers leading God's people into a famous victory. But what are we to learn from such a story? And what does it mean for us today?

Applying 2 Chronicles 20—getting it wrong

This is the only time in the Old Testament that we read of an army going into battle and being led by the choristers. So this was hardly a regular event. Even so, we might still be tempted to conclude that as we go forth in battle for the Lord, like Israel, we should have our church singing group at the forefront of our army of witnessing volunteers. But do we have here a precedent to tune up our guitars, blow out the cobwebs from our saxophones, and tinkle the ivories of our piano accordions as we march into the plenary session of the Global Atheists Convention, singing, 'Shine, Jesus, Shine'? Well, we need to just pause for a moment before we jump too quickly from 800 BC to the 21st century AD.

A moment's reflection will tell us that there is obviously a great deal that is different between Israel's situation back under the old covenant, and our context today. As Christians, we are not a political nation under a monarch like David or Jehoshaphat. We are a people drawn from every tribe and tongue, members of different political entities. Our king is the Lord Jesus who sits enthroned in heaven and whose kingdom is "not of this world" (John 18:36). Therefore we don't wage wars in the military sense. We fight against spiritual forces, and our weapons are spiritual ones (Eph 6:10-20). The walls that we lay siege to and try to penetrate and tear down are walls of unbelief and ignorance. We demolish not bricks and mortar, but arguments and lofty opinions (2 Cor 10:5). The enemies we capture are godless ways of thinking, and it is by preaching and explaining the gospel that we wage spiritual warfare. That's why we don't read of Jesus and the disciples singing songs as they walk around Galilee proclaiming the kingdom, or of Paul leading his apostolic band into Athens playing the trumpet.

For all these reasons and more, we can't make a direct leap from Jehoshaphat to today. Scripture isn't telling us that when we are about to go door-knocking, we should necessarily enter the street singing choruses, or that the missionaries we send out should always arrive at their destination singing songs as they walk into the airport terminal.

Applying 2 Chronicles 20—getting it right

So what positively can we say about the application of this incident for us today?

Luke's account of Paul and Silas' experience of imprisonment in Philippi (Acts 16) gives us an answer to this question. Their plight was every bit as desperate as the one recorded in 2 Chronicles. Both men had been severely flogged and, naturally, were in great pain. They were in a filthy inner cell, with their feet fastened in stocks (v. 24). Worse still, they were both due to face court the next day, with the possibility of further flogging or, even, execution. In short, they were locked up, in great pain and facing a possible sentence of death.

Like Jehoshaphat, some 800 years earlier, escape from this situation seemed impossible. Humanly speaking, there was no hope. Nevertheless, Luke records that at about midnight, while they were "*praying* and *singing hymns* to God" (v. 25), there was a great earthquake that unfastened the prisoners' bonds and flung open the prison doors (v. 26). Once again, the Lord fought for his people and won a great victory against all odds.

The songs of Paul and Silas were a clear testimony to their faith, as well as a witness to those around them, including a certain Philippian jailer. But their singing was more than that. In singing one engages the whole person in an expression of praise to God. It is a turning to God, a glorifying of God and a lifting of our eyes to the hills, "from whence cometh my help" (Ps 121:1, KJV). Therefore, to sing praise in the midst of pain and struggle is profoundly God-honouring, personally uplifting, and deeply strengthening. For as we rejoice in our sufferings we actively strengthen our hope.

Singing has profound psychological value. As many a soldier has found, there's something soul stirring about going into battle with a strong, triumphant song on your lips. It strengthens the heart, stiffens the backbone, and puts resolve and determination where there might have been fear and trepidation. It is for good reason that, for centuries, armies have marched into battle behind brass bands. If this is so, how much more important is it that God's people learn to engage in spiritual warfare by singing spiritual songs—songs that praise God in the midst of trial, that prophesy in the face of persecution, that address our fears and counter the devil's lies with the liberating truths of the gospel of God's grace.

A week after 9/11 and the terrorist attack on the Twin Towers in New York, presidents Bush, Clinton, Carter and Ford attended a service of prayer and remembrance. At this service they sang 'The Battle Hymn of the Republic':

Mine eyes have seen the glory of the coming of the
    Lord:
He is trampling out the vintage where the grapes of
    wrath are stored;
He hath loosed the fateful lightning of his terrible
    swift sword:
His truth is marching on.[30]

This famous song was written by Julia Ward Howe, the wife of a prominent abolitionist at the time of the American Civil War. She was visiting a Union camp in 1862 and heard soldiers singing a tribute to the famous abolitionist, John Brown, "whose body lies a mouldin' in the grave". Knowing she liked writing poetry, a friend asked Julia to write some verses more appropriate to the Civil War effort, but to the same rousing tune. She later recalled:

I went to bed and slept as usual, but awoke the next morning in the grey of the early dawn, and to my astonishment found that the wished-for lines were arranging themselves in my brain. I lay quite still until the last verse had completed itself in my thoughts, then hastily arose, saying to myself, I shall lose this if I don't write it down immediately... Having completed this, I lay down and fell asleep, but not before feeling that something of importance had happened to me.[31]

---

30   J Ward Howe, 'The Battle Hymn of the Republic', 1862.
31   Cited in MK Ham, 'How the Woman Who Wrote "The Battle Hymn of the Republic" Influenced America', *The Federalist*, 4 July 2016 (viewed 7 October 2016): www.thefederalist.com/2016/07/04/how-the-woman-who-wrote-the-battle-hymn-of-the-republic-influenced-america

The *Atlantic Monthly* magazine bought Julia Howe's poem for $4, and it soon became the rallying anthem for Union troops. It inspired American soldiers in World War II, as it did civil rights activists in the 1960s.

Julia Howe's song was an expression of her faith in God. Rightly understanding the nature of his kingdom, she knew that the true battle we fight is a spiritual one for the souls of people, and one with eternal consequences:

> He has sounded forth the trumpet that shall never
>   call retreat;
> He is sifting out the hearts of men before his judge-
>   ment seat:
> Oh, be swift my soul to answer him! Be jubilant,
>   my feet
> Our God is marching on.

So, there's nothing unusual about this strategy. As we've already seen, in times of crisis the people of God have lifted their voices in songs of faith and hope. We ought not hesitate to do the same.

Conclusion

In our brief paddle in the waters of Chronicles, we've been reminded of the important teaching and strengthening role that songs of praise play in the lives of God's people.

So, let's make no mistake about it, every gathering of the church contains at least two sermons. The first is delivered from the pulpit and, in prose, expounds, explains and proclaims God's living word. The other sermon is led from the music stand and, in song, reminds, encourages, teaches and admonishes by the same living word of God. How important it is, therefore, that both sermons proclaim the same truth. The Bible warns against false teachers and false prophets, and that warning applies as much to song writers, song selectors, and song leaders, as it does to anyone else entrusted with the task of rightly handling the word of truth.

We've also seen marvellous historical examples of how the faith of God's people, expressed in song, can inform, inspire, sustain, and empower them in times of trial and suffering. When we sing God's praise in the face of persecution we acknowledge before God and each other our frailty and his sufficiency, our weakness and his strength, our dependence upon him and his faithfulness towards us. And, as we rehearse his great and glorious saving acts, we remind ourselves of all that he has done, is doing and will do for us: "Jesus Christ is the same yesterday and today and forever" (Heb 13:8).

5

The song of the forsaken (Psalms 42 and 43)

The use of these 'psalms of darkness' may be judged by the world to be acts of unfaith and failure, but for the trusting community, their use is an act of bold faith, albeit a transformed faith. It is an act of bold faith on the one hand, because it insists that the world must be experienced as it really is and not in some pretended way. On the other hand, it is bold because it insists that all such experiences of disorder are a proper subject for discourse with God. There is nothing out of bounds, nothing precluded or inappropriate. Everything properly belongs in this conversation of the heart.[32]

Walter Brueggemann

32   W Brueggemann, *The Message of the Psalms: A Theological Commentary*, Augsburg, Minneapolis, 1984, p. 52.

What do I sing when I'm sad?

Why do we assume that whenever people come to church they are in the mood to sing? Is the simple fact that we find ourselves amongst God's people enough to make us want to forget our problems and sing happy songs? Should we persist in *only* singing songs that suggest all is well with our souls, especially when our own experience, and the experience of many others, tells us otherwise? A few years ago two people were killed at a church in Colorado Springs. The choir at Faith Bible Chapel had planned to begin the next Sunday's service with 'Joy to the World'. However, the local paper, *The Denver Post*, reported what one member of the choir said, "We couldn't do it. There was no joy this morning".[33]

From time to time, all of us will feel the weight of some of the sufferings and struggles of living in a fallen world. There may be the pain of wayward children, the heartbreak of a marriage where love has grown cold, the frustration of struggles at work, retrenchment, physical illness, or the pain of watching, or even experiencing, fires or earthquakes or typhoons that have brought death and destruction to many. Not surprisingly, we don't always feel like singing, "If you're happy and you know it, clap your hands." Indeed, we may feel like singing, "If you're hurting and you know it... confused and you know it... angry and you know it... shed your tears".

As we turn to the book of Psalms it's important to

33 T McGhee, '"No joy" in wake of Arvada tragedy', *The Denver Post*, 9 December 2007 (viewed 7 August 2015): www.denverpost.com/2007/12/09/no-joy-in-wake-of-arvada-tragedy

realize that a great deal of the Psalter consists of songs of lament; songs where the authors honestly and painfully put into words their fears, regrets, doubts and hurts. In fact, 73 of the 150 psalms are laments, either in part or in whole. Why, then, do so few of our contemporary songs present us with the brutal realities of life outside of Eden? Why do we have barely a handful of musical resources that both express these sufferings and help us find strength and comfort by turning our hearts and minds to God?

Theologian Carl Trueman suggests one reason for this failure:

> Now, one would not expect the world to have much time for the weakness of the psalmists' cries. It is very disturbing, however, when these cries of lamentation disappear from the language and worship of the church. Perhaps the Western church feels no need to lament—but then it is sadly deluded about how healthy it really is in terms of numbers, influence and spiritual maturity. Perhaps—and this is more likely—it has drunk so deeply at the well of modern Western materialism that it simply does not know what to do with such cries and regards them as little short of embarrassing. Yet the human condition is a poor one—and Christians who are aware of the deceitfulness of the human heart and are looking for a better country should know this.
>
> A diet of unremittingly jolly choruses and hymns inevitably creates an unrealistic horizon of expectation which sees the normative Christian life as one triumphalist street party—a theologically incorrect and pastorally disastrous scenario

in a world of broken individuals. Has an uncon-
scious belief that Christianity is—or at least should
be—all about health, wealth, and happiness silently
corrupted the content of our worship?[34]

In order to help us to respond more honestly to life in a fallen
world let us spend a few moments with a suffering psalmist
who invites us into his world of doubts and desolation.

What is so special about Psalms 42-43?

It is very likely that Psalms 42 and 43 were originally one
psalm. There is no opening ascription to Psalm 43, and in a
number of Hebrew manuscripts they are joined together.
Moreover, you only have to read the two psalms to see
that they tell one story—the story of a believing man's
profound sense of estrangement from God. Somehow, and
he doesn't really tell us how, he has been cut off from the
presence of God, and longs to be in deep communion with
him once again. Both psalms speak of the same experience
and express the same longing. There are three stanzas and
then the following refrain at the end of each stanza:

> Why are you cast down, O my soul,
>   and why are you in turmoil within me?
> Hope in God; for I shall again praise him,
>   my salvation and my God. (42:5-6, 11; 43:5)

But these two psalms don't just belong together. By their

---

34   CR Trueman, 'What Can Miserable Christians Sing?' in *The Wages of Spin:
Critical Writings on Historical and Contemporary Evangelicalism*, Christian
Focus Publications, Fearn, 2004, pp. 158-9.

placement in the Psalter they are marked out as being especially important. First, they are the opening psalms of the second 'book' of Psalms.[35] The significance of this is that the first psalm in each 'book' serves as a kind of introduction to that 'book'. They are also the first of the psalms of the Sons of Korah (Psalms 42-49, 84-85, 87-88), a collection of psalms that speak of either the significance of Mount Zion or the sufferings and longings of God's people; or, as is the case in Psalms 42-43, both themes together.

The message of Psalms 42-43
When will I see you again, God? (42:1-5)

Psalm 42 begins with one of the most powerful and evocative images in the Bible. As the psalmist seeks to describe the aching that he has for God, he selects an image that the people of his time and culture could well understand. It is that of a deer panting desperately for life-giving water. The psalmist feels like an animal that now finds itself lost in the wasteland, cut off from the rest of the herd and removed from the source of water, which is the source of life.

That same sense of desperation for the true source of life, God, has gripped this Old Testament saint. Whatever has happened to him—and we'll learn a little more in just a moment—he is in a situation where he has lost a sense of the presence of God. It is not his sin that has cut him off from God. He is a godly man, a worship leader amongst his people (v. 4), who now senses the Lord's abandonment.

35 The Psalms are comprised of 5 discrete 'books'. Book 1: Psalms 1-41; Book 2: Psalms 42-72; Book 3: Psalms 73-89; Book 4: Psalms 90-106; Book 5: Psalms 107-150.

In the next verses (vv. 3-4) we are given the first hint of the man's situation. For some reason he finds himself far from home, far from Jerusalem, the city of the living God, the location of God's temple. Later in the psalm (v. 6) he talks about remembering the Lord from the land of the Jordan and the heights of Mizar. He feels acutely the fact that he can't participate in the worship that takes place in the temple.

It may be very hard for us to appreciate this religious attachment to a place. We see it with Muslims who in their millions make pilgrimage to Mecca, and Hindus who bathe in the River Ganges. But for Jews the attachment to Jerusalem was much deeper than that. Jerusalem was more than just a sacred site: it was the chosen dwelling place of God on earth (Pss 76:2, 84:1, 132:13).

Excursus: Experiencing God in the old and new covenants

One of the perennial questions that many Christians have pondered is how we should think about the difference between an Old Testament believer's experience of God, and the experience of believers who live after Pentecost. Were David and Solomon, Elijah and Elisha, Ezra and Nehemiah indwelt by the Spirit just as we are? Were they 'born again'?

There is clearly something different about the new covenant. Since Pentecost ushered in a brand new era (with the outpouring of the Holy Spirit), it would be very strange if our experience of the Spirit were identical to that of godly men and women under the old covenant. On the other hand, how could they be truly godly (or even believe!) apart from the work of the Holy Spirit? Scripture is clear that no 'natural' person—then or now—can trust, love and obey

God. In fact, aren't we, even right now, writing about and learning from the psalms of old covenant believers? Don't we feel that their songs are our songs too, precisely because the sentiments they express are our sentiments? Weren't the psalms written by people inspired by the Holy Spirit?

So then, how do we best articulate the similarities and differences between the spiritual experience of old and new covenant believers?

One thing is clearly the same. The faithful under both covenants were and are regenerate. Old Testament believers, just like us, were brought to faith and new spiritual life by the Spirit. Only men and women made alive by the Spirit of God can be truly called 'spiritual', and clearly these old covenant believers were 'spiritual'; they were people who trusted, obeyed and pleased God. "Have you considered my servant Job?" the Lord asks Satan, "a blameless and upright man, who fears God and turns away from evil" (Job 1:8). Job was clearly regenerate.

But there's a very important difference too. Under the new covenant, God's people are permanently indwelt by the Spirit. By him, the Father and the Son have made their home in us (John 14:15-23). Therefore, we know the ongoing presence of the triune God. As we sit in this room in Melbourne working on this book we are in God's presence because his Spirit is in us. If we travel overseas, even to a city where there might not be a single church and which is full of Hindu temples, we are still in the presence of God, for the Spirit of Christ continues to live within us. And that is the experience of every Christian. For "anyone who does not have the Spirit of Christ does not belong to him" (Rom 8:9b).

The reason for this, as we'll see further below, is that Jesus has now fulfilled the function of the temple of which Psalms 42-43 speaks. For, as the New Testament makes plain, he is now the new place of worship where God is fully revealed to us and we are fully reconciled to him. More than that, "as you come to him, a living stone", writes Peter, "you yourselves like living stones are being built up as a spiritual house, to be a holy priesthood, to offer spiritual sacrifices acceptable to God through Jesus Christ" (1 Pet 2:4-5). In other words, when we trust in Jesus, we not only *come to* God's new temple, we actually *become part of* that new temple. That's why it is impossible for a Christian to be separated from the presence of God.

This, however, was not the experience of Jewish believers under the old covenant. Nor was it the experience of the writer of Psalms 42-43. Although the steadfast love of the Lord remained with him (Ps 42:8), in a very real sense he was cut off from the presence of God and the place of true worship.

Back to the psalmist

It is little wonder, then, that as his taunters pose the mocking question, "Where is your God?" (42:3, 10), his deep longing is to go to the temple in Jerusalem. For although God is "a great King over all the earth" (47:2), and is present in every part of his creation (139:7), if you wanted to truly meet with God, at this point in salvation history, you had to go to his house (42:4). For only on Mount Zion, the temple mount, could his saving and sanctifying presence be experienced (42:2). This is why being brought back to God's holy mountain is the psalmist's great hope and prayer:

Send out your light and your truth,
    let them lead me;
let them bring me to your holy hill,
    and to your dwelling. (Ps 43:3)

In light of this, we can understand why their exile in Babylon and the destruction of the temple were so devastating to the Jews. Perhaps we can also understand why Jesus' words, spoken in the second (rebuilt) temple, were so earth-shattering, epoch-making and radical: "Destroy this temple and in three days I will raise it up" (John 2:19). For Jesus was announcing that the era of the Jerusalem temple was now finished. It was no longer the place one should go to meet God. For "he was speaking about the temple of his body" (John 2:21), He was, in effect, announcing: "I am the new temple. I am now the dwelling place of God. If you want to encounter God and experience his presence, you must come to me." That's why Jesus told the Samaritan woman that "a time is coming when you will worship the Father neither on this mountain nor in Jerusalem... the true worshippers will worship the Father in the Spirit and in truth" (John 4:21, 23, NIV).[36]

36 What does Jesus mean by this? The answer from John's Gospel could not be clearer. In line with Old Testament hopes (e.g. Ezek 47:1), the Spirit is the gift that will flow out from the new temple and bring life to God's people. Jesus (as the new covenant temple) is the one who is able to dispense the gift of the Spirit, the "living water" (John 4:10, 7:38-39). Moreover, as the incarnate Word, who perfectly reveals God, Jesus is full of truth (John 1:14) and is the truth itself (14:6). Later in John's Gospel the intimate relationship between the Spirit and Jesus is further emphasized by the fact that Jesus calls him "the Spirit of truth" (16:13), because he will bring glory to Jesus by revealing the truth about Jesus (16:14-15). Clearly then, to worship God "in the Spirit and in truth" is to worship God in and through Jesus and by the Holy Spirit, whom Jesus gives to all who believe in him.

But that day has not come yet for the psalmist. That's why he longs to return to Jerusalem where, once again, he would "lead them in procession to the house of God... with glad shouts and songs of praise" (Ps 42:4). It's because he can't do this that his soul is downcast within him (42:5).

Why have you forgotten me, God? (42:6-11)

The second stanza of the psalm continues in the same vein. The abandoned soul looks down on waterfalls, the springs that gush down from the River Jordan, and rather than being moved by their beauty and their power, they simply serve as a symbol for how he feels. His experience is like someone who has been overwhelmed by the events of life (vv. 6-7). Yet throughout the whole crisis he never ceases being faithful to God. He prays and he sings (v. 8).

Back in 1991, Mike's brother-in-law was kidnapped and spent six months in captivity. He sustained himself during those days of isolation and uncertainty by singing over and over some 600 choruses and hymns he'd learned as a child. Similarly, the writer of Psalms 42-43 nourished his troubled soul by meditating on the songs he had sung in the procession to the temple.

Still, for all that, the taunts and the questions, the doubts and distress remained (42:9-10). As they did for Mike's brother-in-law. During his captivity he kept a diary, and at one point he wrote:

Day followed monotonous day. Some changes seemed to be for the worse. Some for the better. Every day— and many times during the day—I have cried to God for deliverance. Thankfully some days have passed so pleasantly that I had hardly a pain in my heart from being a captive. How many times have I cried, "O Lord, how can I last another day?"

It is not at all uncommon for God's children to feel this kind of fatigue and to express this kind of anguish. Nor is it uncommon for them to sing in the midst of it and to sing about it. Indeed, as was the case with Mike's brother-in-law and as we saw at the end of our last chapter, singing is one of the ways in which God sustains us in the midst of such turmoil. One of the reasons he has given us the gift of song is because singing helps us process pain and awaken hope. Not surprisingly, the threefold refrain (42:5-6, 11; 43:5) ends with a call to hope:

Why are you cast down, O my soul,
    and why are you in turmoil within me?
Hope in God; for I shall again praise him,
    my salvation and my God.

The return of hope (43:1-5)

The third and final stanza (43:1-4) begins with the songwriter pleading with God for vindication in the face of "an ungodly people" and to be rescued "from the deceitful and unjust man" (v. 1). Clearly, there continues to be an immensely painful tension in his experience. On the one hand, he knows that God is his "refuge". But, on the other, he believes himself to be "rejected" by God, since he continues to experience the "oppression of the enemy" (v. 2).

Nevertheless, he has reason for hope. He knows full well, as the refrain testifies, that the Lord is his Saviour and his God. Therefore, he knows that once the Lord has answered his prayer, the desire of his heart will be fulfilled and, like the deer, he will find his "flowing streams"; that is, he will find "the living God" himself (42:1-2). In practice this means he will return to God's "holy hill" (43:3), and again be in the presence of his God, "my exceeding joy" (43:4).[37] Then, naturally, he will do what all true worshippers do when they are full of joy: he will sing praise to God.

If such a response could be true of Old Testament believers whose experience of God's presence was mediated through old covenant shadows (the blood of goats and bulls offered in an earthly sanctuary), how much more should it be true of those whose experience of God's presence has been mediated through new covenant realities (the blood of Christ offered in heaven itself)? That is why joyful singing and heartfelt thanksgiving have always been, and in the world to come will be even more so, a necessary and spontaneous response to knowing the release of God's forgiveness and the reality of his goodness. That is why a church that makes little of music and singing is such an anomaly.

After six long, hard months, Mike's brother-in-law was released from his captivity and he wrote a simple song:

> God has the upper hand, no matter what the plans
>   of man.
> He rules and reigns supreme and does his will.
> Just trust his sovereignty, and you'll not discouraged be,
> But live each day with joy, and worship him.[38]

---

37 Behind the expression "exceeding joy" lie two Hebrew terms, *simcha* and *giyl*, both of which are affectionate and exuberant words, expressing the intimacy and excitement that come from a genuine, saving encounter with the living God.

38 J DeHart, 'God Has the Upper Hand', 1991.

Songs of the Saints

Learning from the psalmist
The abandoned soul

Through the window of Psalms 42-43, we have peered into the experience of one man, deeply sorrowful because he sensed that God had abandoned him. This experience, as we have already noted, is not unique. Even under the new covenant, in which we have the promise of Jesus' never-failing presence (Matt 28:20), we sometimes sense more an absence than a presence. That is not entirely surprising as we live by faith and not by sight (2 Cor 5:7), and God's ways are still, to us, often mysterious and perplexing (Rom 11:33-34).

But as we read this psalm we must not forget that there was one man who entered into the experience the psalmist here describes, and did so in such a way that even the psalmist himself could never have imagined it. Jesus experienced a sense of abandonment by God that was truly unique. In Gethsemane he prayed, "My soul is very sorrowful, even to death" (Matt 26:38). Can't you hear an echo of Psalm 42 in those words? Of course, this foreboding of abandonment became, for the Lord Jesus, an excruciating, existential reality on the cross. For here, as 'the Father turned his face away', the Son cried out in heart-wrenching, soul-searing anguish: "My God, my God, why have you forsaken me?" (Mark 15:34; cf. Ps 22:1).

Dietrich Bonhoeffer was right: if we want to truly understand any of the psalms, "we must not ask first what they have to do with us, but what they have to do with Jesus Christ".[39] First and foremost, then, the lament of

---

39   D Bonhoeffer, *Psalms: The Prayer Book of the Bible,* Augsburg Fortress, Minneapolis, 1974, p. 14.

Psalms 42-43 points forward to the Lord Jesus. No-one has ever known what it is to thirst for the living God as he did on the cross (John 19:28). Indeed, he thirsted for us that we might be forever satisfied!

Learning hope in the dark

By the same token, no-one has ever known hope like the Lord Jesus Christ. He knew the truth of Psalm 42:8: "By day the LORD commands his steadfast love, and at night his song is with me, a prayer to the God of my life." We see this in the telling words he spoke to his disciples on the night of his betrayal: "The hour is coming, indeed it has come, when you will be scattered, each to his own home, and will leave me alone. Yet I am not alone, for the Father is with me" (John 16:32).

Even while he cried out, "My God, my God..." he knew exactly how the story would end. His prayer would be heard, and he would be saved from "the mouth of the lion" and "the horns of the wild oxen" (Ps 22:21). Like the writer of Psalms 42-43, he would once again sing God's praise in the midst of the congregation, telling of the Lord's name to his brothers and sisters (Ps 22:22).

Singing under the new covenant

As we have seen, one of the consequences of Jesus' fulfilment of the Old Testament is that *he* is now the new covenant temple. For this reason, all of us who are 'in Christ' are permanently in God's presence. Consequently, worshipping God under the new covenant can and should happen anywhere and everywhere, not only when we meet together (Rom 12:1-2). There is no designated holy place for serving the Lord (John 4:23-24). Everywhere we go we are in the presence of God, and so wherever we are we can respond to God in prayer and declare his greatness in praise. Unlike the writer of Psalm 137, we can sing the Lord's song in a foreign land (v. 4)—any land!

More than that, singing under the new covenant must inevitably mean that our songs are informed by the rich gospel truths of the new covenant. Yes, we should still sing the psalms—as the apostle Paul encourages us to do (Col 3:16; Eph 5:19), but what we see as in a shadow under the old covenant, we now see in glorious brightness under the new. Our songs, therefore, should be full of Jesus. Full of praise to the Lamb of God. Full of declaring the wonderful works of Christ: his life, death, resurrection, ascension, present reign and future return. Our songs, as much as our sermons, should teach and proclaim the great truths of the faith. We should both celebrate and announce justification by faith, the gift of the Holy Spirit, our adoption and sanctification, and so much more. New covenant believers should not only sing new covenant songs, but be filled with new covenant confidence. For nothing "will be able to separate us from the love of God in Christ Jesus our Lord" (Rom 8:39).

Songs of sadness, songs of praise

The difference between old and new covenant faith, however, must not be over-stated. For instance, it would be a mistake to think that old covenant worship was so focused on the temple activities that it had nothing to do with the rest of life. Nor should we think that a relationship with

God could not, in any sense, be experienced outside of the temple precinct. Even though the psalmist longs to be back in Jerusalem, he can still say: "By day the LORD commands his steadfast love, and at night his song is with me, a prayer to the God of my life" (Ps 42:8).

It is important for us to realize, then, that the 'now but not yet' experience of the psalmist is not entirely different from our own. Yes, we have been saved, but we have been saved in hope. Consequently, tears will often be our food day and night as we "groan inwardly", eagerly but patiently awaiting our full and final redemption (Rom 8:23-24). Lament, then, will also be a normal part of Christian experience. For the message of the gospel is not that Jesus suffered for us, therefore we need never suffer. To the contrary, we will only "share in his glory" if we first "share in his sufferings" (Rom 8:17, NIV).

The importance of lament is not that it makes our troubles disappear, but that as we come before the throne of God and give voice to our present distress, hope is awakened and we are enabled to "rejoice in our sufferings" (Rom 5:3-5). While we wait for the end of our sufferings, singing has a unique way of helping us process the emotional dimension of our pain and so bring us to a point of genuine praise.

Countless saints through the ages have experienced this, and as a result have given the church some of its most profound and enduring songs.

The laments of Christians

Horatio Spafford (1828-1888) was a wealthy and successful Chicago lawyer. In 1870 the Spaffords suffered the tragic loss of their young son. Then on 8 October 1871, almost every property they had invested in was destroyed in the Great Chicago Fire. In 1873, Mrs Spafford and their four daughters left on a boat for Europe, in part to recuperate from these tragedies. Horatio stayed behind, as his business was still reeling from its terrible losses. Just a few days into the voyage, Spafford received word that the ship had been involved in a collision and, while his wife had survived, all four daughters were lost.

On the boat over to join his heartbroken wife, as he passed the very place where his daughters had perished, Spafford wrote the words of the now famous hymn:

> When peace, like a river, attendeth my way,
> When sorrows like sea billows roll;
> Whatever my lot, Thou hast taught me to say,
> It is well, it is well with my soul.[40]

Henry Francis Lyte (1793-1847) was an Anglican clergyman who served nearly half his life as the minister of a church on the southwest coast of England. For the last years of his life he suffered from tuberculosis. A few weeks before his death he took a walk along a beach, contemplating the fact that he would soon leave his church and his ministry. When he returned home, he expressed his sorrow and his hope in these famous words:

> Abide with me: fast falls the eventide;
> The darkness deepens; Lord with me abide;
> When other helpers fail and comforts flee,
> Help of the helpless, O abide with me.[41]

40 H Spafford, 'It Is Well with My Soul', 1873.
41 HF Lyte, 'Abide with Me', 1847.

These examples are of older hymns. Where are the modern songs of lament? Sadly, they are few and far between. How do we account for this lack? Could it be that the saints of a bygone era were more willing to stare suffering and death in the face, and then honestly express both their pain and their faith in song? Could it be that they understood, in a way too many contemporary churches do not, that Christian faith is not an escape clause from hardship, but that suffering must come to disciples who follow Christ in a fallen and hostile world? Could it be that they understood, more profoundly than we, the power of the song to teach, admonish and encourage other believers who, like the psalmist, are saying to themselves, "Why, my soul, are you downcast? Why so disturbed within me?"

Of course, there are some contemporary songs of lament. In fact, Rob is the author of one such song. Like all laments, it's a song with a story. Back in late 2000/ early 2001, Rob watched his father battle, and eventually lose his battle, with leukaemia. During the six-month period of his father's illness, Rob read through the book of Psalms several times, meditating deeply on its laments. As he did so, a song of his own began to emerge, a song he was only able to finish after his father had died. Here is the song in full:

I will trust you in the darkness
I will serve you in my pain.
I will worship in the wilderness
And will follow to the end.
For you are the suffering shepherd
And you know your sheep by name.
So I will trust you in the darkness once again.

I'll believe your word of comfort
When the light of life grows dim.
I will heed your voice at midnight
When the tempests rage within.
I will cling to Christ my saviour
Who has borne my sorrow's sting.
And I will trust you in the darkness once again.

O Lord Jesus, Saviour, Brother, Friend,
Come release us, Lord, come back again.

I will praise your name in winter
When the skies are cold and grey.
I will feed upon your promises
And will cry to you each day.
I will lean upon your Spirit
And your word will I obey.
Yes, I will trust you in the darkness come what may.

Repeat Refrain

I will trust you in the darkness,
On your faithfulness depend,
As I long for your appearing
And the day that never ends.
I will glory in the gospel
And your word of truth defend.
So I will trust you in the darkness once again.
Yes, I will trust you in the darkness, O my friend.[42]

---

42   R Smith, 'I Will Trust You in the Darkness', 2001.

The more we learn to genuinely lament our sins and sufferings, and to do so in song, the more we will truly learn to put our hope in God, and so long for that day when we will see him face to face and every hindrance to our praise will be removed forever.

The Second Movement

6

The songs of Hannah and Mary (1 Samuel 2:1-10 and Luke 1:46-56)

The aim and final end of all music should be none other than the glory of God and the refreshment of the soul.[43]

Johann Sebastian Bach

The 'Fifth Evangelist'

Matthew, Mark, Luke and John are often referred to as the four evangelists. But it will surprise you to learn who has sometimes been described as the Fifth Evangelist: Johann Sebastian Bach!

For most of his life the famous 18th-century German composer was the cantor, or director of choir and music,

---

43   Cited in G Wilbur, *Glory and Honor: The Music and Artistic Legacy of Johann Sebastian Bach*, Cumberland House Publishing, Nashville, 2005, p. 1. Although the quote is ubiquitous, the original source is unknown.

of St Thomas' Church in Leipzig. His role was to organize the music and develop and train the choirs for the four principal churches of the city. One hundred and fifty years before, in 1539, Martin Luther had preached in this church and introduced the Reformation into the city. There is a pillar beside the pulpit that commemorates this momentous event. The other famous plaque in the church remembers Bach's ministry in music in the church. Luther, while a famous theologian, was also an accomplished musician. What may not be as well known is that Bach was not just a musical genius but also an effective preacher. But he was a preacher with a difference. Bach preached through the music he wrote for St Thomas' church.

Part of Bach's work at the church was to compose cantatas for the long—up to four hours!—services. Typically, the cantata was connected with the reading of the Gospel and the sermon. Indeed, the cantata served the same purpose as the sermon, namely it was intended to expound and apply the Scripture that had just been read. Often Bach's cantatas were musical expressions of the gospel, beginning with a statement about human sin, leading to the comforting words of grace and forgiveness, and concluding with the implications of the gospel for life. For example, one cantata, 'My Heart Swims in Blood', begins:

> My heart is bathed in blood,
> For now my sins' great brood
> Within God's holy vision
> A monster makes of me.[44]

44   JS Bach, 'Mein Herze Schwimmt im Blut' (English: 'My Heart Swims in Blood'), 1714.

Later, in the third movement, we hear the good news of Christ's atoning sacrifice:

> I lay myself into these wounds now...
> They shall be now my resting place.
> Upon them will I firm in faith be soaring,
> In them content and happy singing.

Concluding a discussion of Bach's cantatas, professor of sacred music, Robin Leaver reflects:

> The music Bach composed was as powerful as any sermon, perhaps even more so! Like all good sermons, his church cantatas are biblically based and theologically structured. Like all good sermons they are intellectually challenging and emotionally persuasive. Like all good sermons, they are well crafted, aesthetically mature, and supremely memorable. Like his Lutheran predecessors, Bach understood the role of music in worship as the living voice of the Gospel that touches both heart and mind.[45]

Here is a superb checklist for any contemporary Christian songwriter. Is the song you have penned for congregational singing...

» biblically based?
» theologically structured?
» intellectually stimulating?
» emotionally persuasive?
» well crafted?

45 RA Leaver, 'Sermons that Sing', *Christian History*, no. 95, 2007, p. 33.

» aesthetically mature?

» supremely memorable?

Bach's cantatas also highlight what makes music such a powerful medium for communicating the gospel: it touches the mind *and* the heart. Of course, good preaching should do that, too (as, indeed, can a well-written book). But music has a clear advantage in this area.

Great songs of faith are rich in theological truth and powerfully express human feelings and experience. We see this in two of the most important songs in the Bible.

Nothing to sing about

The book of 1 Samuel is the story of Israel's 'fresh start'. The story picks up where the thoroughly depressing book of Judges leaves off. The nation is in a state of moral bankruptcy. She is constantly at the mercy of the marauding Philistines. She is economically marginalized. All in all, she is a rather insignificant loose confederation of tribes, ruled by a series of judges, who increasingly distinguish themselves by their moral and spiritual compromises with the pagan nations around them. But all that is about to change. And the change begins with a young woman who has nothing in her life to sing about.

The books of Samuel open by introducing us to a man called Elkanah, who had two wives. One wife had children and the other, Hannah, had none. In any age and any place childlessness is a deep, deep grief for a woman. But to make matters even worse for Hannah, the other wife delights to taunt and humiliate her because of her barrenness.

So, here is a woman who is helpless. She is completely without the resources to do anything about her tragic condition. She is the object of ridicule from her rival and pity from her husband. Actually, she is the whole nation in microcosm. Israel is helpless, an object of taunting; she is desperate, needy, and overcome by bitterness. Like the barren wife, the nation needs a miraculous divine intervention. Like Hannah, she needs a complete transformation. Both the woman and the nation need the Lord to breathe life into their emptiness.

The remainder of the chapter describes how God worked a great reversal to bring life and joy to Hannah. Indeed, the subject of the whole narrative is the Lord. It is the Lord who had closed Hannah's womb (1 Sam 1:5), and therefore the Lord to whom Hannah turns to open it (v. 11). It is the Lord who "remembered" Hannah's prayer (v. 19) and gives her a son. Later, Hannah fulfils her vow and gives the boy back to the Lord because, "I prayed for this child, and the LORD has granted me what I asked of him" (v. 27, NIV).

God puts a song in Hannah's heart

The Lord has heard Hannah's prayer and given her a new life, and what he has done for Hannah, he is about to do for Israel. Peace and prosperity will replace war and deprivation. And at this major turning point in salvation history there is a song. This song is the overture for what will be this nation's Golden Age. It poetically lays the theological foundations, and sets the theological trajectory, for everything that is to follow in Israel's history. In short, the song of Hannah is one of the most important theological statements in the Bible.

As we 'sing' this song, remember we're singing it on two levels. First, it is Hannah's personal testimony to God's saving grace in her life. But, second, it is also Israel's anthem for what the Lord is about to do for all of his people. Many Bible songs perform this double function, as do many of our historic hymns. For example:

And can it be that I should gain
an interest in the Saviour's blood...
My chains fell off my heart was free...[46]

That was Charles Wesley's personal testimony back in the 18th century. It is also our testimony today. And it is the song of the entire Christian church across space and time.

No God like this God (1 Sam 2:1-3)

Hannah begins by exulting in God's character. She doesn't yet tell us why her days of misery are over. All we know is that God has done something amazing for her, and this great work is "salvation" (v. 1). Interestingly, while she will allude to her specific problem of childlessness, she has clearly written this song for *all* God's people to sing. She speaks in general terms of God's saving grace to his people.

Hannah praises God for who he is: "there is none holy like the LORD" (v. 2). He is a rock and a God of knowledge (vv. 2-3). Of course, if the Lord is holy and knows all things, then he knows both the faithfulness of the righteous and the wickedness of the ungodly. And this is where Hannah's

46   C Wesley, 'And Can it Be', 1738.

song is radically different from the songs of today. If she rejoices in the Lord making the poor rich, and giving them the seat of honour (vv. 7-8), she equally reminds God's people, and the listening world, that this same God breaks the bows of the mighty (v. 4), makes the rich poor (v. 5), he both kills and brings to life (v. 6), cuts off the wicked (v. 9) and thunders against his adversaries (v. 10).

Sadly, the world has muzzled the church when it comes to the songs we sing. The world has said to the church that we will tolerate a god who is kind, loving, faithful, merciful, gracious, and generous. But there is no place in our modern world for a God who is holy, pure, righteous, wrathful, bringing judgement and destruction. We'll accept mercy but not justice. We'll embrace heaven but not hell. Obediently, like good citizens, our preachers in their pulpits have acquiesced to this politically correct view of God, and our song leaders have similarly followed suit by writing and selecting songs that conform to the dictates of the world. And what has been the result? Too many churches have embraced the world's intolerance of the God of Hannah.

But, like sermons, songs teach and inspire. If we were to sing songs like Hannah's—and Deborah's and David's and Mary's and the songs of the throngs around the throne in heaven—we would rejoice in the fact that God *both* "brings down to the grave and raises up" (v. 6, NIV). We would teach our children *all* the truth about God, and they would grow up deeply loving him and appropriately fearing him. We would inspire one another to proclaim to the world the gospel it needs to hear, not just the one it wants to hear.

Singing the gospel (1 Sam 2:4-9)

Hannah's song celebrates the truth that God is the God of reversals, the one who confounds the ways of the world. She catalogues the mighty warrior (whose weapons are broken), the wealthy (who are left beggars), the mother of many (who is rendered childless), and the rich (who is impoverished), while the feeble, the hungry, the barren and the poor take their places. This is what the New Testament calls the gospel. It is the good news that sinners are declared righteous. The enemies of God are called the children of God. The last are made first. Those who were once 'no people' are now God's people. Those dead in their sins are alive in the Spirit. Hannah reminds God's people that it is all God's work: the Lord knows, the Lord kills, the Lord brings to life, the Lord makes poor and rich, he raises up, he guards, he cuts off, he breaks into pieces, he thunders, he judges, he gives strength.

Praise King Jesus (1 Sam 2:10)

The song ends with a line, the full meaning of which Hannah could barely have anticipated:

> "...he [the LORD] will give strength to his king
> and exalt the horn of his anointed." (v. 10)

Of course, when Hannah wrote this song there was no king in Israel. But she looked forward to the day when a Spirit-empowered king would rule over his people, and God would exalt this king above all other kings. In fact, she calls this king the *messiah*, the "anointed" one. Maybe she was thinking that this king might be her son, Samuel.

The author of the book knew she was really singing about David, the boy her son would one day anoint as king. We know that when the Holy Spirit inspired this song in the mind and heart of this young woman he was speaking of the true Messiah, King Jesus.

Another song

At the beginning of Israel's new start a woman sang a song. And at the beginning of another new start for Israel, and indeed the world, another woman sings a song.[47] For 2000 years the church has sung a song called the *Magnificat* (from the Latin *magnificat anima mea, Dominum*, or 'my soul magnifies the Lord'), the song of a young woman who, like Hannah, was given a firstborn son by the Lord. Hannah ended her song singing about how one day God would exalt the power of the Messiah. A thousand years later it is almost as if Mary picks up just where Hannah left off, and rejoices that she will, indeed, give birth to the very child that Hannah sang about.

Actually, the resonances between these two songs are too strong to be coincidental. Clearly, as Mary composed

47 Attentive Bible readers will have noticed that Hannah's 'song' is preceded by the words, "Hannah prayed and *said*" (1 Sam 2:1), and Mary's 'song' by the words, "Mary *said*" (Luke 1:46). Why then refer to either as 'songs'? The answer is, partly, historical: the words of both women have been turned into canticles and sung in various forms down through the centuries. However, behind this phenomenon lies the fact that both Hannah's prayer and Mary's praise are laden with parallelisms and other poetic features that are common to psalms of thanksgiving. For this reason biblical scholars routinely classify them both as 'hymns'. This doesn't necessarily mean that either Hannah or Mary sang their words, but they are certainly given to us in poetic form, a form that naturally lends itself to being sung.

her song, in her mind she went straight to 1 Samuel 2, and she sang her song as a deliberate echo of Hannah's:

» Both songs begin with the singer magnifying God.
» Both songs rejoice in God's holiness.
» Both songs celebrate the Great Reversal: how God brings down the mighty from their thrones and lifts up the lowly.
» Both songs are personal testimonies to God's kindness and mercy.

But where Hannah's song is, implicitly, a description of what the Lord has done for Israel as a whole, Mary's song makes that explicit:

"...he has helped his servant Israel,
      in remembrance of his mercy..." (Luke 1:54)

Mary knows that the son God will give to her will bring blessing to the whole nation. And that, of course, is the other difference between the two songs. Both spoke of the Messiah, the King of Israel, but Hannah spoke of such a ruler not really knowing who she was talking about, while Mary's child was this very one about whom Hannah sang.

Bearing in mind Robin Leaver's comments about the characteristics of Bach's songs, how does the song of Mary measure up?

Biblically based

One commentator describes Mary's song as "a virtual collage of biblical texts".[48] We have seen the deep connec-

---

48   JB Green, *The Gospel of Luke*, NICNT, Eerdmans, Grand Rapids, 1997, p. 101.

tions between Mary's song and Hannah's, but the biblical roots of Mary's song run even deeper than that solitary passage. The song resonates with themes that recur in many of the other songs of the Bible, notably the songs of Miriam, Deborah and Asaph.

The God whom Mary magnifies is the God who reached down in history, again and again, to save his people. Her opening line, in which she rejoices in God her saviour, calls to mind and celebrates all the stories of God's saving mercy. This same theme is picked up in verses 50-51 as she reminds us of God's never-ending mercies throughout Israel's history.

And the song ends on a note that takes us back to the beginning of God's covenantal relationship with his people: all that he has done in salvation has been in order to honour his promises to Abraham (Gen 12:1-3). In short, this wonderful song gives us the Bible's story in a nutshell; we span the history of Israel from Abraham, to whom the promises of blessing were first made, and then to their climax in the Lord Jesus, in whom all these promises find their fulfilment (2 Cor 1:20).

Theologically structured

Mary was understandably utterly overwhelmed at the news the angel had brought to her: that she would be the one who would bear the Son of God. She could have been forgiven if her song had only extolled her wonder at God's grace to her, but this young woman is too theologically informed to dwell on God's grace to her personally. Very quickly she moves to seeing God's grace to her as exemplifying how he has always acted in human history. He has always responded with kindness to those who fear him (Luke 1:50), he has always been the God who delights to dwell with the humble (vv. 51-52), and he has always acted mercifully when his people have been in need (v. 54). The theological implication of Mary's song is that this God is the same, yesterday, today and forever. It is a profound exposition of deep theological truths. In other words, this magnificent song is really a theological commentary on both the significance of the Christ-event that Luke is narrating, and the wider history of God's people.

Intellectually stimulating

Not surprisingly, Mary's song has been the subject of serious research and reflection—theologically, poetically, and even politically.

On the theological front, not only does the song's sweep encompass the whole of redemptive history, but through it we are introduced to many of the key themes of Luke's two-volume work: Luke-Acts. In particular, the themes of God's might and mercy, his salvation of the humble and judgement of the proud, riches and poverty, and God's faithfulness to the promises made to Abraham, all find their first echoes in this poem. Moreover, the fact that this is *Mary's* song highlights the importance of women in God's saving purposes—both as recipients of his blessing and partners in his work.

On the poetic front, Mary's song, in both form and content, appears to be patterned on the 'hymns of praise' found in the book of Psalms. Thus, the opening lines display a familiar feature of Hebrew poetry: synonymous parallelism. For example, "my soul" (v. 46) mirrors "my spirit" (v. 47), and "magnifies the Lord" (v. 46) matches with "rejoices in God my Saviour" (v. 47). The final lines, likewise, contain a series of contrasting parallels: the proud are scattered, the rulers brought down, the humble lifted up, the hungry filled, the rich sent away empty.

On the political front, in the past century there have been a number of instances of governments banning the public recitation of the *Magnificat*. For example, it was not allowed to be read or sung during the time of British rule in India. The reason? Its message was regarded as too politically subversive. The German theologian Dietrich Bonhoeffer saw this clearly, as the following words from his 1933 Advent sermon reveal:

This song of Mary's is the oldest Advent hymn. It is the most passionate, most vehement, one might almost say, most revolutionary Advent hymn ever sung. It is not the gentle, sweet, dreamy Mary that we so often see portrayed in pictures, but the passionate, powerful, proud, enthusiastic Mary, who speaks here. None of the sweet, sugary, or childish tones that we find so often in our Christmas hymns, but a hard, strong, uncompromising song of bringing down rulers from their thrones and humbling the lords of this world, of God's power and of the powerlessness of men. These are the tones of the prophetic women of the Old Testament: Deborah, Judith, Miriam, coming alive in the mouth of Mary.[49]

49   D Bonhoeffer, *The Collected Sermons of Dietrich Bonhoeffer*, ed. Isabel Best, Fortress Press, Minneapolis, 2012, p. 116.

Emotionally persuasive

It is difficult to account for the popularity of this song on the basis of its theological maturity alone. Its appeal is intensified by the fact that it is a real, open-hearted, ecstatic expression of joyful praise. Mary is overwhelmed by God's kindness and mercy to her. She is an insignificant village girl, and yet the mighty God has looked upon the humble condition of his servant (v. 48). Mary not only understands God's unfathomable mercy, she *feels* its immensity, and this emotion expresses itself in unbounded joy. Every verse reverberates with gladness and gratitude. The tone is set by the opening lines where she sings that her soul and spirit magnify and rejoice in all that God has done for her. Having set this joyful tone, Mary melodically continues to praise God by demonstrating, both in her own life as a microcosm, and the history of the nation as a whole, how God has always remembered and saved the humble.

Well crafted

Structurally, the song of Mary is a carefully crafted piece of poetry. For example, Mary makes extensive use of chiasms:[50]

A ...he has brought down rulers from their thrones
B and exalted those of humble estate;
B he has filled the hungry with good things
A and the rich has sent away empty. (vv. 52-53)

50 A chiasm is a style of writing (often used in ancient literature) that employs a particular structure for clarification and/or emphasis. In a chiasm, a series of ideas is expressed in a particular sequence. These ideas are then followed by the same (or similar) ideas in the reverse sequence.

And thematically, it is skilfully structured. One writer has described Mary's song as an "appealing tapestry".[51] Like the song of Hannah, it interweaves her own experience of salvation with God's wider expression of mercy to Israel. For example, just as God has regarded the lowly condition of his bond slave Mary (v. 48), he has similarly shown unceasing mercy to his servant Israel (v. 54). Further, as the Lord has done great things for this young woman in appointing her to bear the Messiah, so, by implication, pious Israel, from whom the Messiah will come, will have a glorious future as she, too, is exalted (v. 52) and filled with good things (v. 53).

Aesthetically mature

It has been reliably claimed that the song of Mary has been set to music more than any other hymn or canticle in the history of the church. Almost every great composer of music for the church has written music for this song (e.g. Monteverdi, Vivaldi, Bach, Bruckner, Rachmaninoff, John Rutter Thomas Tallis, Ralph Vaughan Williams, Herbert Sumsion, Charles Wood and John Tavener). This is a testimony both to its importance amongst the songs of Scripture, as well as to the force and beauty of its structure and language.

51 DM Casey, Jr. 'Mary's Magnificat', *The "Holy Land": Quarterly of the Franciscan Custody of the Holy Land*, 1999 (viewed 7 October 2016): www.christusrex.org/www1/ofm/mag/MAen9909.html

Supremely memorable

From at least the 5th or 6th centuries, the *Magnificat* has held pride of place in the liturgies of both the Western and Eastern churches. Often on a daily basis, Christians have sung one of the many versions of this song for 1500 years, and in many churches around the world it continues to be sung every Sunday. There have also been a number of contemporary adaptations of it, either in part or in whole. For example, Rob's own song, 'Great Things' (co-written with Mike Begbie), picks up a number of key themes from the song, marries them with the gospel events that Mary's words anticipate and turns the opening lines of her song—"My soul magnifies the Lord, and my spirit rejoices in God my Saviour"—into a memorable chorus for all God's people to sing:

> David's great descendant, Mary's blessed child,
> Lived to raise the humble, died to reconcile.
> Mercy upon mercy, freeing us from shame,
> By his precious life-blood, sinners he reclaims.
> Blessed be his name
>
> *Chorus*
> O my soul magnifies the Lord,
> And my spirit rejoices in God, my Saviour.
> My soul magnifies the Lord,
> For he who is mighty has done great for me.[52]

---

52 R Smith and M Begbie, 'Great Things', 2012.

Learning from Hannah and Mary

One of the great benefits of living in a globalized world is that Christians are well aware that they are not alone. While the church in the West may bemoan the decline in adherence to the Christian faith, and the growing opposition to Christian belief, it can take great heart from the fact that in other parts of the world the church is growing in unprecedented numbers. Further, those churches that are presently spared from persecution can support and pray for others who are suffering for their faith in Christ. Never before, has the church been as conscious of the fact that it is a body as wide as the world itself.

By contrast, many contemporary Christians conscious of their links geographically with believers of other places, have never been less conscious of their links historically. We can feel our connection with those across space, but may sense little connection with those across time. We recognize that we are one with those of other nations, but have little cognizance of the fact that we are one with those of other times.

Hannah and Mary did not suffer from this same myopia. Hannah's song brought to mind not only what God would do for her and her people in her own day, but also spoke prophetically of what he would do for future generations through the anointed King who would come. Mary's song, while rejoicing in God's mercy to her personally, sings of his mercy "from generation to generation" (v. 50). She is deeply conscious of her connection to the historic nation of Israel.

Mary's song is the first song of the New Testament. In many ways, it is the first song of the new covenant. No song has been sung by the church longer, or probably more frequently, than the *Magnificat*. For 2000 years the church has sung, with Mary, "My soul magnifies the Lord", and in singing this song we join together with the saints across the centuries in praising the same Saviour God. We join our voices in an expression of common worship.

Of course, most Christians are largely ignorant of Church history, and have little awareness of the great events of their past. We give little thought to the achievements and trials of those who came before us. However, there is one way we can express our unity with them: the fact that we are one in hope and faith and doctrine. We can do that by singing the songs that have been our heritage, and God's gift to us from the beginning. It has been a mark of wisdom that many churches today remember and rehearse the song of Mary. By all means, contemporize the music (as Rob and Mike Begbie have done), but this great song not only gives us a marvellous example of a wonderfully rounded Christian song, but in singing it we are united with our fellow believers in ages past.

7

Psalms, hymns and spiritual songs (Ephesians 5:18-21 and Colossians 3:15-17)

Let me encourage you, Christian people, to sing a great deal more than you do. Of old London, in the Puritan time, it was said that you might have heard songs and prayers in well-near every house as you walked at the breakfast hour from St. Paul's to Eastcheap. Family worship was then the prevailing custom! It would not be so now in any town in England—the more the pity.[53]

CH Spurgeon

53   CH Spurgeon, 'Blessings Manifold and Marvelous', sermon no. 3474, published 2 September 1915 (viewed 6 October 2016): www.spurgeongems.org/vols61-63/chs3474.pdf

People of the Song

Charles Spurgeon encourages Christians to sing more, even when we gather as families. But what about our corporate gatherings? How much time should we give to singing? How many songs should we sing? Mike and Rob attend different churches in different cities, and visit lots of churches around the world. They asked each other about their own experience with congregational singing.

Mike's answer: We attend the oldest church in my city. It is traditional, liturgical and evangelical. Singing is a very important part of the service. The central event of our gathering is the exposition of the Bible, and the theme of the particular text of Scripture shapes the content of much of the rest of the service, especially the music. Each Sunday the congregation sings four hymns, all expressing important themes from the Scripture that is being expounded. The church also has a small, but very gifted, choir who sing four anthems, one at the beginning of the service, one before the first of our four Bible readings (yes, four Bible readings!), one right after the sermon, which rehearses the main point of the sermon, and one during communion. So, there are eight songs, all deeply steeped in the Bible and profound, edifying theology. My church is a singing church and I love it!

Rob's answer: If I think of our evening service, we typically sing four or five songs at each gathering. One or two at the beginning, one before the sermon, one after the sermon, and one at the end. Often the opening song contains a 'call to worship', exhorting us to give God our praise for all he's given to us. 'Come, People of the Risen King', by Keith and Kristyn Getty and Stuart Townend, is a good example of a helpful opening song, and one we sing regularly. The songs before and after the sermon are usually closely related to the theme or content of the sermon itself—although sometimes the song before the sermon might be in the form of a prayer asking God to give us ears to hear and hearts to obey. The final song is usually designed to remind us of the gospel and send us out to serve God in the world. Obviously, there are lots of variations to this pattern, but that's the general shape. All told, our singing together would regularly take up about a quarter of our time together.

From its very inception, the Christian church has been a singing church. But *what* exactly should Christian people sing, particularly when they gather together? Should the church sing only Scripture or, as some have argued, only the Old Testament psalms? Or is it legitimate to sing words that are not direct scriptural quotations but are consistent with Scripture?

Many Christians also remain confused about *why* we should sing. What do we think we're doing when we sing together as a church? Is singing primarily an act of worship or praise offered to God? Or do we sing to encourage and edify other believers? Or, is it both? In this chapter we'll explore how the New Testament answers these important questions, and we'll do so by focusing on two key passages.

Psalms, hymns and spiritual songs: What are they?

On two occasions, Ephesians 5:19 and Colossians 3:16, the apostle Paul calls upon Christian congregations to engage in singing "psalms and hymns and spiritual songs". But what exactly is he referring to?

The case for 'exclusive psalmody'

There has been a strong tradition stemming from some branches of the Reformation to some churches today that regards the terms 'psalms', 'hymns' and 'spiritual songs' as only referring to the three types of psalms found in the Psalter. The implication of this view is that the church should sing nothing other than the biblical psalms. The principle behind this is that only those practices that are clearly instituted by biblical command, precept or example are permissible in corporate Christian worship; *everything else is prohibited*.

While you will not find many people in the contemporary church pushing this line, it still boasts a few passionate advocates. For example, the Rev. Hugh Cartwright, formerly a Professor at the Free Church of Scotland College, argues the case forcefully:

> We cannot just assume that "psalms, hymns and spiritual songs" are to be understood according to the modern usage of these words. These terms must be understood according to their biblical usage. It has to be said that the Greek words *psalmois, humnois, odais* translate the Hebrew words *mizmorim, tehillim, shirim* and that these are the terms used in

the Book of Psalms and of the various contents of the Book of Psalms. Indeed, *tehillim* is the term used to describe the Book itself, the Book of Hymns. There is no doubt regarding the place given in Old and New Testaments to the divinely inspired Psalms and there is no-one who can prove that the passages in Ephesians and Colossians refer to materials of praise outwith the Book of Psalms, and certainly not to material not inspired by the Spirit.[54]

Without calling into question the strengths and benefits of singing the Old Testament psalms (which, as we've seen, are many!), we need to assess the validity of this interpretation of "psalms and hymns and spiritual songs". The best way to answer this question is by looking at how New Testament writers, and Paul in particular, use these three terms.

'Psalms' in the New Testament

Apart from its use in Ephesians 5:19 and Colossians 3:16, the Greek term *psalmos* appears on five other occasions in the New Testament (Luke 20:42, 24:44; Acts 1:20, 13:33; 1 Cor 14:26). The instances in Luke and Acts quite clearly refer to the Old Testament psalms. In 1 Corinthians 14:26, however, it appears alongside "a lesson, a revelation, a tongue, or an interpretation". As Gordon Fee points out, the gifts listed "mostly likely... represent various types

---

54   Taken from an address entitled 'The Regulative Principle', given to the Inverness Branch of the Scottish Reformation Society, 14 February 2000. The substance of the address can be found online entitled, 'Does the Bible tell us what to sing?' (viewed 7 August 2015): www.fpchurch.org.uk/about-us/how-we-worship/exclusive-psalmody/does-the-bible-tell-us-what-to-sing

of verbal manifestations of the Spirit". He therefore concludes that "since the last three are Spirit-inspired utterances, and therefore spontaneous, it is likely that the first two are to be understood in that way as well".[55]

However, given the important role the psalms played in the preaching of the apostles, and the number of times Paul quotes them in his writings, it would be surprising if the psalms did not play a similarly important role in the communal singing of the early Christians. At the very least, these factors suggest that "psalms" in Ephesians 5:19 and Colossians 3:16 includes the Old Testament psalms, though perhaps not exclusively.

'Hymns' in the New Testament

In the New Testament, the noun 'hymn' (Gk. *hymnos*) appears only in Ephesians 5:19 and Colossians 3:16. The verbal form, however, occurs on four occasions (Matt 26:30; Mark 14:26; Acts 16:25; Heb 2:12). The references in Matthew and Mark almost certainly refer to the singing of one or more of the 'hallel psalms' (Psalms 113-118), given that traditionally these were sung in conjunction with the Passover meal. In Acts 16:25 Paul and Silas are "singing hymns to God" while in prison, but we are not told what they were singing. Hebrews 2:12 quotes Psalm 22:22: "I will tell of your name to my brothers; in the midst of the congregation I will sing [a hymn to] your praise." Again, we're not told if the 'hymn' to be sung is another of the Old Testament psalms or some other song of praise.

55   GD Fee, *God's Empowering Presence: The Holy Spirit in the Letters of Paul*, Hendrickson Publishers, Peabody, 1994, p. 690.

The very fact that Paul appears to distinguish this kind of song from "psalms" in Ephesians and Colossians suggests that the two terms are not completely synonymous. In fact, some scholars are convinced that the New Testament itself gives us examples of these 'hymns' (e.g. Phil 2:6-11; Col 1:15-20; 1 Tim 3:16). Mind you, Paul never introduces these passages by calling them 'hymns'; so this, too, is uncertain.

'Spiritual songs' in the New Testament

What then of "spiritual songs"? Here we are on firmer ground. In addition to its appearance in Ephesians 5:19 and Colossians 3:16, the word 'song' (Gk. *odē*) appears five times in the book of Revelation (5:9, 14:3[x2], 15:3[x2]). In each case it refers not to a citation from the book of Psalms, but to a song of joy offered in praise of God and the Lamb (Jesus) and the victorious salvation they have won for us.

However, in our two passages Paul adds the word 'spiritual' (Gk. *pneumatikos*). In other places in his writings, 'spiritual' simply means 'of the Spirit'. So, for example, Paul refers to "spiritual gifts", those gifts that the Spirit himself distributes (1 Cor 14:1). He likewise speaks of "spiritual people", men and women indwelt and taught by the Spirit (1 Cor 2:15). In similar fashion, "spiritual songs" seems to refer to songs that were freshly inspired by the Spirit and so were, quite possibly, spontaneous in character.[56] If this is correct, "spiritual songs" is another way of talking about the kind of song he calls a "psalm" in 1 Corinthians 14:26.

56   ibid., pp. 653-4.

What, then, shall we sing?

What, then, are we to make of all this? Given the flexibility of the terms 'psalms', 'hymns' and 'spiritual songs' in the New Testament it is difficult to sustain the case that Paul uses all three terms exclusively of the canonical psalms. Taken together, "psalms and hymns and spiritual songs" seem to cover the whole range of Christian congregational singing, from canonical psalms (at one end) to spontaneous songs (at the other). Therefore, without wanting in any way to disparage the historic practice of psalm singing, to limit our singing to only the Old Testament psalms is unnecessarily restrictive of the freedom Christians have been granted under the new covenant. Of course, anything and everything that is sung by God's people ought to be brought to the bar of Scripture, that its truthfulness and helpfulness might be assessed. If a song (whatever its pedigree) is 'agreeable to Scripture' and communicates the truth of God's word with clarity, then God's people should be free to make use of it. But if a song is disagreeable to Scripture and confuses the truth of God's word, then God's people are obliged to reject it.

Psalms, hymns and spiritual songs: Why sing them?

Now we turn to the very important question of "Why?" To what end did the New Testament church sing "psalms and hymns and spiritual songs"? What was their purpose? The best way to answer this question is by looking more closely at Ephesians 5:19 and Colossians 3:16 in their contexts.

The answer of Ephesians 5:19 in context

We need to begin with the immediate context of Ephesians 5:19. Paul writes:

> And do not get drunk with wine, for that is debauchery, but be filled with the Spirit, addressing one another in psalms and hymns and spiritual songs, singing and making melody to the Lord with your heart, giving thanks always and for everything to God the Father in the name of our Lord Jesus Christ, submitting to one another out of reverence for Christ. (Eph 5:18-21)

The key thing to note here is that there is one command in these verses: "be filled with the Spirit" (v. 18). By the use of 5 participles ("addressing", "singing", "making melody", "giving thanks" and "submitting"), Paul then fleshes out this command. But how do we understand the relationship between the command and the participles? Commonly, people have seen the participles as describing the *result* of being filled with the Spirit. In others words, when a church is filled with the Spirit certain activities flow from this spontaneously. One of the marks of being a Spirit-filled church, then, is that the congregation will sing psalms and hymns and spiritual songs.

Whilst this interpretation has many merits, and may well be true in practice (i.e., when God's people are filled with his Spirit, these are the kinds of things that result), it is our view that Paul is here describing the *means* by which he expects the church to carry out the command to be filled with the Spirit. This does not mean that Paul is saying, in some mechanical way, "Do these five activities and—hey presto—then you'll be Spirit-filled." No, but just as the Lord has given us personal 'means of grace' whereby we can grow as Christians, so he has given his gathered people communal 'means of grace' so we might be spiritually nourished together.

Actually, while most modern Bible translations use the phrase "filled *with* the Spirit", Paul probably meant us to be "filled *by* the Spirit".[57] But, if so, filled with what? Or with whom? The answer is found in Ephesians 3:16-19, where Paul shares his prayer that through the Spirit's empowerment, Christ might dwell in his readers' hearts so that they "may be filled with all the fullness of God" (v. 19). He then goes on to describe the gifts that Jesus has given to each one so that the church can become mature and grow into "the measure of the stature of the fullness of Christ" (4:13). This is why it is vital to maintain the unity of the Spirit (4:3) and not to grieve the Spirit (4:30), so that the Spirit can accomplish his work of filling us all with Christ and so with God the Father.

This is also why Paul's command, "be filled", is in the 'second person plural'. It is a *corporate imperative*. In other words, he's not talking here about one's own individual walk with the Lord or growth in personal piety (as essential as these things are). Rather, because the one Spirit has created one body (4:4), made up of "beloved children" (5:1), spiritual growth is a family affair. The end goal of

---

57   So the Holman Christian Standard Bible and the NET Bible. Interestingly, the Young's Literal Translation has "be filled *in* the Spirit". As the Greek preposition *en* can mean 'in', 'with', or 'by', all of these translations are possible and the differences between them negligible. But for contextual reasons, and also the parallels with Colossians 3:16, we are persuaded that 'by' is to be preferred.

being filled is that the church "be so 'full of God' by his Spirit that our worship and our homes give full evidence of the Spirit's presence".[58]

Furthermore, like the command to "walk by the Spirit" (Gal 5:16), Paul's injunction to "be filled by the Spirit" is not a matter of 'letting go and letting God', but a matter of active obedience to the will of God (Eph 5:17). But how does Paul expect the church to carry out this command? Thankfully, we're not left to guess; the 5 participles spell out the 'means of grace' by which the Spirit continually fills the church.

To draw the obvious conclusion, then, singing "psalms and hymns and spiritual songs" is a vital means not only of addressing one another (thereby edifying the church) and making melody to the Lord (thereby praising Christ), but of being filled by the Spirit with all the fullness of God (Eph 3:19). That singing will also be the result of such a filling is not only logical but also the common experience of God's people. Indeed as the history of revivals has often demonstrated, where the Spirit of God is there is also singing. It is even possible that Paul's thought may contain a certain circularity: the singing of the saints leads to Spirit-filling which leads to singing and so on.

However, his focus on "addressing", "singing", "making melody", "giving thanks" and "submitting" as *means* of being filled by the Spirit should not be missed. They highlight our responsibility to "look carefully" at the way we walk (5:15), they guide as to how to make "the best use of the time" (5:16) and they give us understanding of "what

58   Fee, *God's Empowering Presence*, p. 722.

the will of the Lord is" (5:17). The first four, in particular, accentuate the importance of congregational song for the life and health and growth of the church. Why this is so, is spelled out with even greater clarity in Colossians 3:16.

The answer of Colossians 3:16 in context

Again, we need to start by seeing the immediate context of Colossians 3:16:

> And let the peace of Christ rule in your hearts, to which indeed you were called in one body. And be thankful. Let the word of Christ dwell in you richly, teaching and admonishing one another in all wisdom, singing psalms and hymns and spiritual songs, with thankfulness in your hearts to God. And whatever you do, in word or deed, do everything in the name of the Lord Jesus, giving thanks to God the Father through him. (Col 3:15-17)

Again, the context of these verses, as with Ephesians 5, is a corporate one. In the entire passage Paul's focus is the Christian community: its unity, harmony, corporate thankfulness and, in particular, its *one another* ministry.

Paul's primary concern is that "the word of Christ" (the message of the gospel) might dwell richly among the members of the body of Christ. But how is this to happen? Again, we are not left in the dark. Believers are to teach and admonish one another in all wisdom. But what form is this teaching and admonition to take? No doubt, it could (and did) take any number of forms—from public preaching to private conversation. But Paul's thought here is that it takes place *by means of* singing psalms, hymns and spiritual songs.[59] Paul is, therefore, highlighting the God-given potency of "psalms and hymns and spiritual songs" to enable a rich indwelling of the life-giving "word of Christ". Of course, he is not suggesting that the role of teachers in the Christian community is now redundant, any more than he is suggesting that singing together does away with the need for preaching or the reading of Scripture. Put positively, Paul's point is simply that congregational singing ought to be regarded as a serious and powerful form of 'word ministry'.

In light of this, it is little wonder that Paul regards singing as a means of being filled by the Spirit (Eph 5:18-19). For to be indwelt by the word of Christ is not a different experience from being "filled by the Spirit". You can't separate Christ from his word or Christ from his Spirit. Paul is, therefore, expressing the same reality in two different ways. What this means is that as we sing the word of Christ to one another more is happening to us than we often realize. Yes, we are being instructed and growing in wisdom. But, as a community, we are being filled with the fullness of God. For to be filled with the word of Christ, is to be filled with the Spirit, to be filled with the Spirit is to be filled with Jesus, to be filled with Jesus is to be filled with God. This takes place every time we sing "psalms and hymns and spiritual songs" to one another with gratitude in our hearts to God. Such is the power and wonder of congregational singing.

59   D Moo, *The Letters to the Colossians and to Philemon*, PNTC, Eerdmans, Grand Rapids, 2008, p. 288.

It is also important to consider the word "richly" in Colossians 3:16. Why does the apostle add this word? Evidently, it is possible that churches may let Christ's word dwell in them poorly or ineffectually (or not at all!), perhaps by singing songs which do not clearly convey "the word of Christ" or, more likely, by singing them 'half-heartedly', without a profound sense of thankfulness to God or the intention of actively encouraging others. This should not be! We could not put it more robustly than did John Wesley:

> Sing lustily and with good courage. Beware of sing-
> ing as if you were half dead, or half asleep; but lift
> up your voice with strength. Be no more afraid of
> your voice now, nor more ashamed of its being
> heard, than when you sung the songs of Satan.[60]

The importance of two-dimensional singing

At the beginning of this chapter we posed the important question: Why do we sing? Our two passages give us the same answer. Congregational singing is two-dimensional: it is both *God-directed* as an act of glorification (the vertical dimension) and *one another-directed* as an act of edification (the horizontal dimension).

On the vertical front, both passages exhort us to sing and make melody to the Lord Jesus, giving thanks to God the Father in his name. Indeed, God-directed gratitude is a major theme, Paul urging the Colossians to thankfulness

---

60   J Wesley, from his 'Preface' to *Select Hymns with Tunes Annext* ('Sacred Melody'), s.n., London, 1761.

three times in as many verses (Col 3:15-17; cf. Eph 5:20). On the horizontal front, both passages likewise call upon us to address or teach and admonish one another in song. As Martin Luther liked to stress, it's in singing that the congregation becomes the preacher and preaches to itself!

The 'take-home' message is clear: only when congregational singing is focused on *both* the glory of God *and* the good of others, does it fulfil the powerful purposes for which God has given it to us.

And yet we can separate them and, consequently, err in one of two directions in our singing. First, *we can fail God* by being neglectful of his glory. Once again, John Wesley was very much aware of this danger and so urged: "Have an eye to God in every word you sing. Aim at pleasing him more than yourself, or any other creature."[61] To sing only to others is to break the first commandment and could even earn us Jesus' chilling rebuke: "I never knew you" (Matt 7:23)! So like the psalmist we should pray to the Lord for an undivided heart that we might truly fear his name, give him wholehearted thanks and desire to glorify his name forever (Ps 86:11-12).

Second, *we can fail others* by being neglectful of their good. There was a popular chorus a few years ago that contained the lyric, "Let's forget about ourselves and concentrate on him, and worship him."[62] Certainly, make the Lord the object of our singing, but we must *not* forget about each other. Perhaps the song wasn't suggesting we should. Whatever the case, we must only sing and make melody to the Lord in ways that ensure the "upbuilding

61   ibid.
62   BT Ballinger and H Leonard, 'We Have Come Into His House', 1976.

and encouragement and consolation" of the church (1 Cor 14:3). For to praise God in a way that is unedifying to others is defective worship at best and will rob the congregation of the full richness of being filled by the Holy Spirit with the word of Christ. This is simply an application of 1 John 4:20 to congregational singing: "for he who does not love his brother whom he has seen cannot love God whom he has not seen."

Conclusion

We have already made the point that a congregation hears two sermons whenever they gather together: one proclaimed from the pulpit, the other from the music stands. We must ensure that we both turn our thoughts and affections to the God and Father of our Lord Jesus Christ, and faithfully teach and edify the congregation. Therefore, we must ensure that, just as we entrust the pulpit to the wise and mature, we similarly entrust the music microphones to those who know the God of the gospel and understand the purpose of the important ministry they exercise.

Of course, it's possible to overstate the importance of Christian congregational singing. It's not the only, nor is it the central, means by which Christ is building his church. But it's also possible to understate its importance and so to fail to properly appreciate its God-given purpose. Singing together is one of the means by which the church of Christ is filled by the Spirit with the fullness of God. This happens as the saving and sanctifying word of Christ dwells richly among his people. This, in turn, happens as we heartily praise God and address one another in "psalms and hymns and spiritual songs"—that is, in songs of all kinds that faithfully convey the truths of Scripture. We undervalue the significance of this ministry at great cost to our life and health as God's people. The verdict of JC Ryle, therefore, still needs to be heard today:

> Good hymns are an immense blessing to the Church of Christ. I believe the last day alone will show the world the real amount of good they have done. They suit all, both rich and poor. There is an elevating, stirring, soothing, spiritualizing, effect about a thoroughly good hymn, which nothing else can produce. It sticks in men's memories when texts are forgotten. It trains men for heaven, where praise is one of the principal occupations. Preaching and praying shall one day cease forever; but praise shall never die. The makers of good ballads are said to sway national opinion. The writers of good hymns, in like manner, are those who leave the deepest marks on the face of the church.[63]

63 JC Ryle, 'Toplady and His Ministry', in *Christian Leaders of the 18th Century*, Banner of Truth, Edinburgh, 1885, p. 382.

8

The songs of heaven (Revelation 4-5)

So far therefore as we sing this song on earth, so much shall we have the [foretastes] of heaven... And this will make our public assemblies some image of heaven, and will make our Sabbath days and thanksgiving days some resemblance of that eternal Sabbath and thanksgiving that is solemnized by that innumerable company of angels and spirits of just men made perfect.[64]

Jonathan Edwards

The now and the not-yet

Being a Christian in this world has never been easy. This shouldn't surprise us because Jesus told his disciples that the road of discipleship would be tough: "A servant is not

---

64   J Edwards, 'They Sing a New Song', *Sermons and Discourses, 1739-1742*, ed. HS Stout, *WJE Online Vol. 22*, Jonathan Edwards Centre at Yale University, New Haven, 2008, p. 241.

greater than his master. If they persecuted me, they will also persecute you" (John 15:20). The Lord, then, could not have been clearer: suffering and opposition are the norm for God's people in this age. That is the reality of living in the 'now'. Glory, rest, and vindication are coming, but they belong to the 'not-yet'.

Of course, compared to many in the world today, the persecution of Christians in the highly secularized West is mild and sporadic. But for many Christians living in other parts of the world, the experience of persecution is extreme and unrelenting. Indeed as we write, Christians in Iraq, Syria, Ethiopia, Egypt, Pakistan, Yemen, Nigeria and the Ivory Coast are being shot, beheaded and even crucified for refusing to deny Christ. Still, for all true disciples of Jesus, there will be spiritual warfare (whatever form it takes) and there will be trouble. "If they persecuted me, they *will* also persecute you."

How, then, can struggling servants of Jesus be sustained? What will help us to endure to the end? Is there any way to find joy in the journey of following Christ and strength in our suffering for the sake of his gospel?

The Jesus who warned us of the persecutions to come has also given us the resources we need to endure, and indeed rejoice in, these hard times. There is much in his word, the Bible, to give us comfort, hope and strength. In particular, the book of Revelation is written with that specific aim in mind. The apostle John who brings this revelation to us introduces himself as, "your brother and partner in the tribulation and the kingdom and the patient endurance that are in Jesus" (Rev 1:9). John has words from God for us that will keep us loving and worshipping the Lord Jesus, no matter what our enemies throw against us. If ever there was a book written for the persecuted church, it is this one.

It's called 'Revelation' because it contains a revelation from Jesus Christ given to the apostle John while he was imprisoned on the island of Patmos for his Christian witness. However, the revelation wasn't just given for John's sake alone, but "to show to his servants the things that must soon take place" (Rev 1:1; cf. 22:6). John identifies with his fellow believers who are facing opposition from the authorities of their day. But more than that, the words of this book are also written for Christians of every place and every age, that we all might understand who really is in control in a world that is so hostile to the Lord Jesus and his people.

But why are we talking about these things in a book on music and singing? The answer is that one of the ways in which the book of Revelation administers its potent message is through the presentation of songs—heavenly songs. In the pages that follow, we're going to examine just two of those songs: those found in Revelation 4 and 5.

Needless to say, these chapters are a small part of the larger 'revelation'. But they are a key part, for in them John is given access to the heavenly throne room, and shown a vision of God the creator in all his majestic glory and Jesus Christ the redeemer in all his saving grace. More than that, John enjoys the privilege of seeing and hearing the praises of the heavenly host, as they both reveal and extol the wonder and glory of the person and the works of God and the Lamb!

So, as we read the words of these heavenly hosts, we need to keep before us the purpose of these songs. Yes, they remind us of what God has done and the wonder of his saving grace, but these eternal truths have a very practical and pastoral purpose. The curtain is stripped back and the volume is raised so that as we, in a sense, see and hear the heavenly hosts at worship, our own faith can be encouraged and fortified. Like us, John was suffering in the 'now' and patiently waiting for the dawning of the 'not-yet'. The visions he saw of God and the Lamb, and the songs he heard praising their power and majesty enabled him to understand the nature of reality and to find comfort in the knowledge that God is in control and will bring history to its ordained end. These visions and songs are designed to bring to us the same joy, comfort and strength. So, let's look and listen carefully.

The one who is seated on the throne: Revelation 4

Revelation 4 opens with a breathtaking vision of God in all his sovereign majesty, transcendent glory and resplendent power. Before him is the Holy Spirit, pictured as seven fiery torches, and around him are twenty-four elders, probably angelic beings. John also sees creatures that resemble a lion, an ox, a man, and an eagle. So, we have animals, birds and human beings, representing the various facets of the created order. And what are they doing? They're glorifying God. In other words, they are doing what all creatures were designed by their creator to do: giving unceasing praise to their eternal, all-powerful master and maker. They call out constantly: "Holy, holy, holy, is the Lord God Almighty, who was and is and is to come!" (Rev 4:8)

Strictly speaking, John describes the creatures as 'saying' this song of praise, but it's generally understood that, in fact, they are saying by singing.[65] The song they sing evokes a memory of Isaiah's vision of the seraphim gathered around God's throne, similarly calling out, "Holy, holy, holy is the LORD of hosts" (Isa 6:3). But the song of Revelation 4 says even more: God is worthy of all the glory because he transcends time and history. Nations and rulers come and go, but the Lord reigns forever. God has plans and purposes that stretch from one end of eternity to the other, and this eternal God will ensure that these plans are fulfilled.

The song, then, is asking a question of all those who will listen: Whose side will you be on and to whom will you entrust your future? Will you give your allegiance to the unholy, ephemeral, transient earthly rulers? Or will you serve and worship the holy, eternal, sovereign king of heaven and earth? It's in seeing such a vision, and both hearing and participating in the chorus of all creation around the throne, that God's people can be empowered to persevere faithfully through tribulation. This, then, is a song that needs to be heard!

65 Singing, of course, is a form of speech that augments regular speech with tonality and rhythm, and so can quite appropriately be described as saying. But is that what's happening here? A number of clues given in the following chapter would suggest as much. In 5:9 we read, "And they sang a new song, saying..." This verse helps answer our question in three ways. First, mention of a "new song" being sung in the heavenly courts suggests the singing of earlier songs. Second, the song to Christ the redeemer (which follows) most naturally stands in contrast with the song to God the creator (in chapter 4). Third, this "new song" is also described as being 'said'—suggesting that the earlier words of acclamation (in chapter 4) were said by being sung. Further arguments could be added, but the vision of God communicated by the 'song' is even more significant than whether it was said, chanted or sung.

The song of the twenty-four elders (vv. 9-11)

Nor are the living creatures alone in giving God praise. In his vision, John sees others joining their choir:

> And whenever the living creatures give glory and honour and thanks to him who is seated on the throne, who lives for ever and ever, the twenty-four elders fall down before him who is seated on the throne and worship him who lives for ever and ever. They cast their crowns before the throne, saying:
>
> "Worthy are you, our Lord and God,
>   to receive glory and honour and power,
> for you created all things,
>   and by your will they existed and were created."
>   (Rev 4:9-11)

Once again, all those created beings gathered in God's presence see his eternal glory. He is the one who lives forever and ever. Spontaneously, they fall down on their faces in perpetual wonder, adoration, thanksgiving and praise. The God who created all things and sustains them in their existence, and who sits enthroned in heaven, is truly worthy to receive all glory, honour and power.

This eternal God is worshipped because there is nothing in all creation that exists apart from his will and purpose. From the mightiest Roman emperor to the pygmy shrew, the smallest known animal on earth, all exist because of the will of God. He reigns supreme over all things, and even now there is a realm where his glory is endlessly acknowledged and his will is always done (as the Lord's Prayer reminds us).

What's more, the existence of such pure worship and perfect praise in the heavenly court is the guarantee that one day on earth God's eternal purposes will be fulfilled, and then the whole earth will join with heaven and be filled with the knowledge of his glory as the waters cover the sea (Hab 2:14).

It should be apparent why this is such an important vision for suffering Christians to see, and such a necessary song for persecuted believers to hear. We all need to be reminded that God is in control of his creation. When times of trouble and hardship come, we can be tempted to think that, either God has abandoned us, or perhaps he has turned a deaf ear to our troubles. Maybe darkness will triumph? Perhaps the gates of hell will prevail against God's church? No, these heavenly beings see things as they really are. God is ruling. His plans for his people and his creation, which stretch from eternity, will come to pass. One day he will receive the glory, honour, and power that is his due. So, we have nothing to fear.

But before we pursue these thoughts further, there is a major question that needs to be answered. If God's plans are on track, how are they being worked out? How will the 'now' become the 'not-yet'? The answer is found in the second part of John's vision, and a second song, recorded in the next chapter.

The Lion who is the Lamb: Revelation 5
Who is worthy to open the scroll? (vv. 1-5)

In the vision that opens chapter 5, John sees a scroll. The following chapters of the revelation tell us that this scroll contains all God's plans for the judgement and salvation of the world he has created, and every single human being will be caught up in these great end-time events. The angel therefore asks, "Who is *worthy* to open the scroll?" (v. 2) In other words, who is pure, righteous, just, and wise enough to reverse the curse that lies over this world and its inhabitants? John's despair at the apparent lack of such a person is short-lived. One has been found who is truly worthy. One of the elders says to him: "Weep no more; behold, the Lion of the tribe of Judah, the Root of David, has conquered, so that he can open the scroll and its seven seals" (v. 5).

We are now given a wonderfully paradoxical vision of this triumphant person. He is "the Lion of the tribe of Judah". This title harks back to a prophecy that Jacob announced concerning his son, Judah, who he likens to a lion. But more than that, Jacob also promises that one of his descendants will be the ruler of the nations. He declares:

> "Judah is a lion's cub...
> The scepter shall not depart from Judah,
>   nor the ruler's staff from between his feet,
> until tribute comes to him;
>   and to him shall be the obedience of the
>   peoples." (Gen 49:9-10)

The Lion of Judah is the promised son of David, the great king of Israel, descended from the tribe of Judah, whose kingdom would be established forever (2 Sam 7:12-13). The elder then reveals to John that this 'Lion King' has defeated the enemies of God (Rev 5:5). The doom of those who oppress God's people is therefore certain. He is truly the King of kings and Lord of lords (Rev 19:16)!

The Lion who is the Lamb (vv. 6-10)

John has been told *that* the Lion King has already won the decisive victory, but not *how*. John's next revelation is as stunning as it is surprising:

> And between the throne and the four living creatures and among the elders I saw a Lamb standing, as though it had been slain, with seven horns and with seven eyes, which are the seven spirits of God sent out into all the earth. And he went and took the scroll from the right hand of him who was seated on the throne. (Rev 5:6-7)

John sees a vision of the Lord Jesus, reigning as King, but forever bearing the marks of the death by which he conquered sin, death, and Satan. This all-powerful Lamb (hence the seven horns) also possesses and sends into the world the Holy Spirit (the seven spirits of God) who brings to fulfilment God's saving plans (v. 6). It is no surprise, given this awe-inspiring vision, that:

> the twenty-four elders fell down before the Lamb...
> And they sang a new song, saying,
>
> > "Worthy are you to take the scroll
> > > and to open its seals,
> > for you were slain, and by your blood you
> > > > ransomed people for God
> > > from every tribe and language and people
> > > > and nation.
> > and you have made them a kingdom and
> > > > priests to our God,
> > > and they shall reign on the earth." (Rev 5:8-10)

Here's why the lion of the tribe of Judah is the master of human history who fulfils creation's destiny: it is because, through the sacrificial shedding of his own blood, he has cancelled the curse of sin and so ransomed an international family for God. What's more, this diverse group from "every tribe and language and people and nation", who once lived their lives locked into a cycle of defeat, will one day reign upon the new earth.

No wonder the heavenly choir sings. Yet John tells us they sing a "new song". In what sense is this song 'new'? There is nothing new about singing a new song, for the Bible repeatedly records God's people singing new songs (e.g. Pss 40:3, 144:9; Isa 42:10; Rev 14:3). The reason for such songs is simple: every new display of God's saving power and grace demands a new outpouring of praise and thanksgiving. We've already seen that Exodus 15 sets the paradigm. There are also occasions when the songwriters of the Bible will sing a 'new song', not because God has acted in a new way, but because they want to respond afresh to what God has done in the past to save his people (e.g. Pss 33:3, 96:1, 98:1, 149:1).

But this new song is doubly new. The triumphant saving work of the Lord Jesus, while built on the shadows and prophecies of the Old Testament, is such a stupendous and climactic new work that it demands not only this new song, but a whole cavalcade of new songs. Consequently, these songs aren't just new in that they appeared at this point in time in salvation history, but their substance and character exist on a new plane. A new day of salvation, a new covenant, a new people, a new priesthood, and a new hope demands a new song. And not just one new song; many new songs! In fact, if we were to read on in the book of Revelation we would hear many more 'new songs', extolling all that God has done for us in the Lord Jesus (e.g. 7:10-12, 11:15-18, 12:10-12, 15:3-4, etc.).

What's more, the day of writing such 'new songs' is not over. Every generation will not only want to rehearse the songs of their forebears in the faith, but will necessarily be moved to write their own 'songs of the Lamb'; new songs that celebrate and proclaim the wonderful works of our savior God that have their centre and focus in the crucified and risen Lord Jesus.

The worship of the heavenly hosts (vv. 11-14)

The praise of Revelation 5 is like an avalanche. Once the mountain begins to shake and move, it gathers an unstoppable momentum. The "four" and "twenty-four" of verses 6-8 are joined by the "many angels, numbering myriads of myriads and thousands of thousands" of verse 11, and finally climaxing with the worship of "every creature in heaven and on earth and under the earth and in the sea and all that is in them" in verse 13. They all with a loud voice ascribe to God and to the Lamb "power and wealth and wisdom and might and honour and glory and blessing!" (v. 12).

Isn't it striking that all creation worships not just "him who sits on the throne" (v. 13) but also the Lamb (vv. 12, 13)? If during his earthly life people spontaneously and appropriately fell down and worshipped Jesus (e.g. the magi in Matthew 2 and the women at the empty tomb in Matthew 28), how much more can we expect all creation, on beholding the Lion King, to join with the four living creatures who said "Amen!" and the elders who fell down and worshipped (v. 14)?

Learning from the songs of heaven

What we are given in these remarkable chapters of the book of Revelation is not only a glimpse of the celestial worship arena, but a window into the control room of history, God's heavenly headquarters. This is the place from which creation's story is being directed, its destiny determined, and the stages of God's great plan of salvation and judgement put into effect.

In being shown such a vision, we see that, despite appearances to the contrary, God is in control. Our world might continue to be plagued by wars and suffering on both individual and national levels, and the church may appear to be relentlessly battered and bruised by those who display their hatred for God in attacking his people, but God's good and wise purposes are right on track, and will not be thwarted. We can be sure of this because there is One who has conquered and by his blood has ransomed people for God from every tribe and language and nation—Iraqi, Israeli, Pakistani, Russian, Chinese, Iranian, Nigerian, Kenyan, German, Italian, English, American, Australian and so on. Moreover, he is still in the process of gathering his people from the ends of the earth, and enlisting all who follow him as partners with him in the fulfilment of his eternal plan.

In light of these unshakeable truths, one clear response these chapters call us to make is to sing. But sing what? Sing why? Sing how? There are at least four important lessons for us to draw for congregational singing from these two chapters.

First, they set before us a goal. Singing is a vital activity of God's people in both this age and the age to come.

The songs of the heavenly choir remind us that while the response that God desires is more than singing, it is not less than singing. A theology of 'song-less' worship is oxymoronic. An appreciation of the mighty works of God and the glory of his Son must issue in an outpouring of celebratory song. If the heavenly hosts sing that God and the Lamb are worthy to receive power, wealth, wisdom, might, glory, honour and blessing then so should we. They deserve our praise. They have earned our honour. All they are and all they have done has more than warranted our worship. Why would we ever want to give them less than the glory that is their due?

Second, they set before us a challenge. If we're honest, our times of congregational singing are sometimes (or more than *some*times) a very poor reflection of the praise we see in Revelation 4-5. They are not always *wonder*ful, but often wonder-less. Our minds are easily distracted. At times, we are emotionally, or even intellectually, disengaged. If we're preaching or service leading, we're thinking about the sermon we're about to preach or the next item in the program. Whatever the reason, our singing—like our praying, hearing of God's word and conversations with one another—can be very perfunctory.[66] By contrast,

66 While we're being honest, the reality is also that sometimes we just don't feel like singing. If my body is wracked by pain or my heart is broken with sorrow or my mind is deeply troubled with anxiety, there may be seasons when prayers are difficult to pray and songs difficult to sing. Ecclesiastes reminds us that there is a time to weep and a time to laugh, a time to mourn and a time to dance (3:4). That means there can be a time to be quiet, as well as a time to sing; seasons of lament as well as seasons of praise. We live in a broken and fallen world and there will be periods in our lives when we feel that brokenness very acutely. These are not places where we want to, or should, remain, but we need to acknowledge this reality.

the living creatures encircling the throne never tire of praising God. Day and night they cry out, "Holy, holy, holy, is the Lord God Almighty" (Rev 4:8).

Third, they set before us a pattern. In these songs we are given a wise template for the content of the songs we are to sing. The songs of Revelation praise God for who he is: the eternal creator who made all things. And they remind us of who we are: creatures who exist and continue to have our being only by his gracious will. We should sing songs that both remind us of who God is, and who we are. We must likewise continue to write the new songs that remind us of the work of the Lion who is the Lamb. The musical paradox is that the new songs we continually need to write must be about the old, old story. You might know the famous 19th-century hymn by Katherine Hankey, 'Tell Me the Old, Old Story':

> Tell me the old, old story of unseen things above,
> Of Jesus and His glory, of Jesus and His love.
> Tell me the story simply, as to a little child,
> For I am weak and weary, and helpless and defiled.

> *Refrain*
> *Tell me the old, old story, tell me the old, old story,*
> *Tell me the old, old story, of Jesus and His love.*

This theologically profound hymn recognizes that we need to hear this 'story' regularly:

> Tell me the story often, for I forget so soon;
> The early dew of morning has passed away at noon.

The hymn writer then reminds us what this old story is:

> Tell me the story slowly, that I may take it in,
> That wonderful redemption, God's remedy for sin

And, like the heavenly songs of Revelation, this earthly song knows that being reminded of the cross of Christ is the best remedy for a life torn apart by sorrow:

> Tell me the story always, if you would really be,
> In any time of trouble, a comforter to me.[67]

Finally, these songs set before us a ministry. Revelation 4-5 implicitly reminds us of the vital service provided by those who lead the singing in our congregations. To the beleaguered church of the first century the songs of Revelation were given to strengthen and encourage them in their faith. By singing such songs and reminding ourselves of these great gospel truths today we, too, can be emboldened to stand firm against temptation and maintain the witness of our lives and our lips in the midst of a hostile society. Through the wise selection of the songs we sing, 'the congregation's other preachers' can help the beleaguered churches of today maintain "the patient endurance that [is] in Jesus" (Rev 1:9).

Conclusion

> "In the world you will have tribulation", said Jesus. "But take heart; I have overcome the world" (John 16:33).

---

67 AK Hankey, 'Tell Me the Old, Old Story', 1866.

What we've seen in this chapter is that the songs of heaven do more than simply point us to the eschatological future; they show us the glories of the heavenly present. The Lamb has already redeemed, already conquered, and is presently reigning at the right hand of God. So there is real reason to take heart. But, in addition to that, the heavenly songs give us a pattern to reflect in the here and now. For the Spirit has been sent out into the world to establish the kingdom of our Lord and of his Christ. The songs of the hosts of heaven, then, should be the songs of the redeemed on earth. That means we need to learn to sing them, and others like them, even in the midst of the trials and troubles of this life, the pains and persecutions that our Sovereign Lord calls us to bear.

The new song of the Lamb has begun. Jonathan Edwards was, therefore, right: "as we sing this song on earth, so much shall we have the [foretastes] of heaven" and in our "public assemblies some image of heaven".[68] So then, by the power of the Spirit, let us join our voices with those of the hosts of heaven, praising our holy creator and gracious redeemer, and doing so all the more as we see the Day drawing near (Heb 10:25).

68 Edwards, 'They Sang a New Song (Rev. 14:3a)', p. 241.

Songs of the Saints

9

Why God's people sing

Music and silence—how I detest them both! How thankful we should be that ever since our Father entered Hell... no square inch of infernal space and no moment of infernal time has been surrendered to either of those abominable forces, but all has been occupied by Noise—Noise, the grand dynamism, the audible expression of all that is exultant, ruthless and virile... We will make the whole universe a noise in the end.[69]

CS Lewis

Why don't we sing?

Mike was at a convention, seated near the rear of the auditorium. The music team at the front were 'leading' (and we use that word advisedly) and we were singing. Well, we were meant to be singing. And so Mike did what he's done quite often lately; he closed his eyes and listened

69   CS Lewis, *The Screwtape Letters*, HarperCollins, New York, 2001, p. 119.

to the singing. The song leaders with their microphones were clear and distinct. One could identify each of the several instruments accompanying the singers. But if you could block out the 'worship team', all that was left was a barely audible murmur around the building. He opened his eyes and looked around. Most people were either standing silently, not even making pretense of singing, or appeared little engaged in the activity. He turned to a friend next to him and commented, "No-one's singing". The man looked at him as if he'd just observed that no-one was flying. "Of course, they're not singing", he said. "We haven't *really* sung here for years." Whatever was happening that morning, it was decidedly *not* congregational singing.

So, what's gone wrong? We travel around and visit many churches, conferences and conventions across the denominational spectrum, and when it comes to singing there is something wrong. Not everywhere. And maybe not where you are. But in too many churches people, by and large, are not singing. Is it because too many of the songs on the screen in front of them are unsingable? Or is it because people have given up trying to compete with drums, two or three electric guitars, keyboards, and three, four or five song leaders with microphones? Whatever the reasons, in many places there's both a clear lack of enthusiasm for, and engagement with, congregational singing. Oh the music is often very loud and skilfully played and the 'worship leaders', as they are now dubbed, are energetic; but vocally where has everyone else gone? We have been in some Christian meetings where, if the congregation were (like the apostle Paul) suddenly and mysteriously raptured to heaven, the song leaders would carry on regardless, blithely unaware they were the only ones singing. Genuine, heartfelt congregational singing has been in its death throes in too many churches for some years now, and we've got to ask why—and what can be done about it.

Hopefully we have convinced you by now that congregational singing is just too important to be left lying in the doldrums. Of course, not everyone would agree with that assertion. For some, the preaching of the word of God is so important that anything else (with, perhaps, the exception of taking up the offertory!) is legitimate but marginal. So, we continue to permit perfunctory singing and, even, perfunctory prayer in our communal gatherings. That we are, in fact, teaching, edifying and admonishing one another, and making melody in our hearts to the Lord seems almost to have escaped attention. Of course, we want to affirm the centrality of reading, hearing and responding to the word of God when the church comes together. But when the place and purpose of congregational singing is properly understood then we see that it is actually an integral part of the ministry of God's word amongst his people.

Surely, all Christians, whether or not we are involved in the church's music ministry, should be concerned to make the singing that takes place in our church as vital, edifying and all-inclusive as possible. The practice of congregational singing is simply too important to allow the malaise to continue.

The enemies of the song

The 'worship wars' are nothing new; they've been raging for centuries. The Puritans who settled in America in the 17th century were embroiled in the 'Controversie of Singing'. A minority argued that when Paul exhorted the Ephesians to sing and make melody *with the heart* (Eph 5:19), then he meant by implication *and not with the voice*. In other words, Christians were not to sing aloud. Of course, that's literalism raised to the level of absurdity, but they went on to argue that if everyone sings, then no-one is listening and so the congregation is not being edified. Some went so far as to stuff cotton wool in their ears so they could not hear the congregation. There have been times when Mike's wife would have liked to stuff cotton wool in his mouth so those around couldn't hear him, but this was more a comment on *his* singing than congregational singing generally!

So, why do we sing? Do we have to sing? If we encourage God's people not to switch off their ears when God's word is being proclaimed, should we similarly exhort them not to keep their mouths shut when we sing? If we become disturbed at a church's apparent lack of responsiveness to the preached word, should we also be concerned at its apparent indifference to its psalms and hymns and spiritual songs?

As we've conceded already, singing serves a number of practical purposes in a church service. We begin with a song to give latecomers a chance to find a seat, ensuring that they haven't missed anything important. Or when a congregation has been sitting down for a while it's good to be able to get up and stretch one's legs—and, perhaps hands also, depending on the kind of church you attend! And it makes a good way to mark the end of the formal part of the gathering and to move outside to greet one another. But is that why we sing congregational songs?

Let us suggest 8 more compelling reasons for why we sing.

Eight reasons to sing
1. The God who sings

One of the more remarkable and delightful verses in the Bible is Zephaniah 3:17:

> The LORD your God is in your midst,
>   a mighty one who will save;
> he will rejoice over you with gladness;
>   he will quiet you by his love;
> he will exult over you with loud singing.

Zephaniah is writing in the days of Josiah, king of Judah (640-609 BC). Josiah was the last, and in some ways, greatest of the good kings of Judah. Indeed, "before him there was no king like him, who turned to the LORD with all his heart and with all his soul and with all his might, according to all the Law of Moses, nor did any like him arise after him" (2 Kgs 23:25). Sadly, just around the corner for Judah was destruction and exile. And this little prophetic book predicts this imminent catastrophe. But, as with all the words of the prophets, even Zephaniah's last word is not judgement, but grace and the hope of restoration. Zephaniah looks forward to the day when God's people, the "daughter of Zion", will "rejoice and exult with all [their] heart" (Zeph 3:14) because God will again stand in their midst, victorious over his—and their—enemies.

And God will sing. But wait a minute, how do we interpret this verse? Is this just a poetic metaphor expressing God's delight at the salvation of his people? Or does God sing? The great Baptist preacher CH Spurgeon was convinced of the latter. In a sermon delivered on 30 October 1887 he said:

> Think of the great Jehovah singing! Can you imagine it? Is it possible to conceive of the Deity breaking into a song: Father, Son and Holy Ghost together singing over the redeemed? God is so happy in the love which he bears to his people that he breaks the eternal silence, and sun and moon and stars with astonishment hear God chanting a hymn of joy.[70]

Spurgeon observes that God did not sing when he made the world. The angels did because creation was very wonderful to them, "but it was not much to God, who could have made thousands of worlds by his mere will. Creation could not make him sing..." And God does not break out in song at his wonderful works of providence, "for he could arrange a thousand kingdoms of providence with ease".[71] So, Spurgeon asks, if it is not creation or providence, what prompts the High King of heaven to sing? And the answer is his work of redemption. When he saw the rescue of his people, especially through the sacrifice

---

70 CH Spurgeon, 'A Sermon for the Time Present', sermon no. 1990, delivered at the Metropolitan Tabernacle, 30 October 1887 (viewed 22 September 2016): www.spurgeon.org/sermons/1990.php
71 ibid.

of his only begotten son, "then he rejoiced after a divine manner".[72]

Yes, "after a divine manner", the Lord God rejoices. It's pointless to speculate what God's singing might be like. So Spurgeon wisely says, "I tremble while I speak of such themes, lest I should say a word that should dishonour the matchless mystery; but still we are glad to note what is written, and we are bound to take comfort from it".[73] In the same vein we can say that God loves "after a divine manner", and God expresses his wrath "after a divine manner". In other words, God's expressions of both mercy and judgement spring from emotions that, while analogous to human feelings, are of quite a different order. In the same way, "after a divine manner" the Saviour God sings.

2. Singing is natural

We were made to sing. No matter how far back you go in human history and no matter how far around the world you travel, you'll find people singing. In fact, unless there's something organically wrong, all children are able to sing and most of their first attempts at speech are singing sounds—after all singing is really just a form of extended speaking. And we all do it, often unconsciously. It may be while driving the car, or taking a shower, or pulling the weeds, but we whistle, sing or hum. Singing is a very normal, natural human activity.

Now that's not to say that all cultures are the same, or that all people are the same. Clearly we're not. Nor is it

72 ibid.
73 ibid.

to deny that some people find singing difficult or embarrassing. It's been estimated that one in four people believe they can't sing—usually because they've been given the message (at a fairly young age) that they were 'off tune', or bellowed, or were 'droners'. But all things being equal, singing is an entirely natural and universal human activity. It is just part of the way we were designed by God to express ourselves and to communicate with him and others. So it is hardly surprising that from the beginning to the end of the Bible we see God's people repeatedly bursting into song.

So, we sing because we can—and only humans can. Animals make their distinctive noises, but only humans have the ability to blend words with a million different melodies. It is natural to sing, and unnatural not to.

3. Singing is healthy

If singing is natural and universal, then, not surprisingly, it is also good for us. It's not only good for us physiologically, but also psychologically. In fact, singing can be defined as a unique form of communication produced by a series of complex muscle-movements set in motion by a fundamentally emotive desire to express beauty, gladness, pain or sadness.

Now what this definition highlights is the fact that singing is bound up with the expression of our emotional life. In fact, there is now an entire school of psychotherapy known as 'singing therapy' because—guess what—people have discovered that through the physical experience of singing suppressed emotions can start to thaw out, which can allow people to then begin to process their inner pain.

An American psychologist, Dr Gene Cohen, claimed that tests had shown that when elderly people sing they then have fewer medical appointments, use less medication, and become less depressed. Of course, since the therapeutic benefits of singing are not age-restricted, the activity can benefit anyone of any age.[74]

One of the sad realities is that many who have histories of trauma or abuse have lost their voices—they can't sing or (at least) don't want to. Now we can understand that; the activity of singing threatens to awaken a part of them that's in very great pain. But unless it is awakened, it can never be healed. That's why singing therapy is one very gentle but effective way of doing just that.

4. Singing aids memory

The memorization of Scripture has been a long-standing Christian practice. And the case for memorization has been strengthened by stories of Christians, often missionaries, who having found themselves in a remote location, without a Bible, have been able to sustain themselves spiritually because they've memorized large portions of Scripture. If devout Muslims memorize the Qur'an, and devout Jews memorize the Torah, how much more, then, should Christians hide God's word in our hearts?

But it doesn't work for everyone. We may believe it's a good thing to do, but some of us just have lousy long-term memories. Many of us can't even remember people's names, let alone Bible references. Perhaps we take comfort

74 GD Cohen et al, 'The impact of professionally conducted cultural programs on the physical health, mental health, and social functioning of older adults', *Gerontologist*, vol. 46, no. 6, Dec 2006, pp. 726-34.

from the author of Hebrews when he writes: "It has been testified somewhere" (Heb 2:6). Memorization can be tough. But put a tune to the verse and everything changes.

Mike was speaking at a conference and, impromptu, decided to take the audience with him on a walk down a musical memory lane. He began to sing the old 'Scripture in Song' classic, 'His Banner over me is Love'. And every proud Baby Boomer immediately joined in—and with the actions. Mike reckons we could have sung dozens of those 1970s 'Scripture in Song' choruses, which we haven't sung in decades, and for most people the words would have come flooding back.

Rob was in a church recently where the projection system failed. But rather than that putting an end to the singing, the congregation members found that most of the words of most of the songs were well and truly embedded in their memories. They therefore needed very little prompting and almost nothing was lost in the quality and fervency of the singing.

We can switch on the radio and listen to a song we haven't heard in 20 years and find ourselves singing along. Of course, that's why so much of the old church liturgies were sung and not spoken. A people who were largely illiterate would remember what they sang.

Both of us have had the experience of conducting services in retirement villages. Many who come along have lost the capacity to concentrate for more than a few moments. As the service proceeds, they drop their heads and close their eyes. Even some who have kept their eyes open have that distant look which betrays that while they are physically present, they are mentally absent. Until we sing. Once the piano plays the opening chords of a familiar old hymn, heads lift, lips begin to move, and smiles break upon their faces. Their recall of the words is remarkable.

One of the great imperatives of Scripture is 'Remember', and one of the great purposes of memorizing Scripture is growth in godliness. As the psalmist writes: "I have stored up your word in my heart, that I might not sin against you" (Ps 119:11). So those over the years who have exhorted us to memorize Scripture have done us a great turn, just as those who have turned Scripture into song have done much to aid our remembering.

5. Singing teaches

Why did the Evangelical Awakening of the 18th century produce so many great songwriters? Under the power of the Spirit the gospel had spread across Britain and North America and gripped the hearts of thousands. But these large congregations of biblically illiterate believers needed to be educated and discipled. It was a calculated strategy to do this both by preaching and teaching and the writing of hymns. Men like Watts and the Wesleys wrote and encouraged hymn singing because they rightly saw hymns as effective vehicles for teaching the great truths of the faith. The hymns not only expressed the personal, saving experiences of these new Christians, they were memorable essays on doctrine.

How powerful songs are as a medium for teaching came home to Mike some years ago when he was the guest preacher at a local church. It was a missions weekend and he was asked to give talks intended to encourage God's people to commit themselves to taking the gospel to the nations. He spoke on Acts 4:12: "...for there is no other name under heaven given among men by which we must be saved". He wanted people to understand and feel the urgency of taking the gospel to all the nations, and so reminded them of Jesus' uncompromising uniqueness as Lord and Saviour. Without Christ people are lost, facing God's terrifying, eternal wrath, and their only hope is the Saviour who gave himself for the sins of the world.

Before the address, we spent about 45 minutes singing choruses, mostly about God's love and faithfulness. How God gently enfolds us in his loving arms, how special we are to him, and how undyingly faithful and committed he is to us. All true, of course. But where was the atonement? Judgement? Heaven and hell? The gospel?

Mike then rose to preach and the clash in both content and tone between the songs and the sermon was obvious to any discerning person there. How could a God like the one we'd just sung about ever judge someone, or demand they believe only in Jesus? On that night two sermons were preached, and they didn't give the same message. As we've seen, songs teach and we must ensure that they teach the gospel clearly and faithfully.

Interestingly, the custom used to be that pastors wrote the hymns. Many would prepare their sermon for Sunday early in the week, and then at the end of the week encapsulate all they wanted to teach in the words of a song. For example, the most famous hymn of all time, 'Amazing Grace', was written by John Newton after he had spent the week reflecting upon 1 Chronicles 17, where the Lord tells King David: "I took you from the pasture, from following the sheep, to be prince over my people Israel" (v. 7).

And David is overwhelmed by God's kindness:

> "Who am I, O LORD God, and what is my house,
> that you have brought me thus far? And this was
> a small thing in your eyes, O God. You have also
> spoken of your servant's house for a great while
> to come, and have shown me future generations,
> O LORD God!" (vv. 16-17)

Newton then asks, isn't that the heart of the gospel? And,
like David, he was stunned by God's amazing grace. A
week's meditation on Scripture was transformed into an
unforgettable song, one that is now indelibly imprinted
on the memories of millions.

6. Singing creates a world

'Baltic voices raised in song to drive out recession blues.'
That was the headline in *The Sydney Morning Herald* on
7 July 2009. The article told the remarkable story of how
singing revolutionized a nation:

> A Singing Revolution brought Estonia blood-free
> independence from the Soviet Union in 1991 and
> now tens of thousands have joined mammoth
> choirs to banish recession blues.[75]

In the past the Estonians used songs instead of weapons
to express their resistance to their Soviet oppressors
during what has been dubbed the Singing Revolution of

75 A Reigas, 'Baltic voices raised in song to drive out recession blues', *SMH*,
7 July 2009 (viewed 7 October 2016): www.smh.com.au/world/baltic-voices-
raised-in-song-to-drive-out-recession-blues-20090706-dafv.html

1988-1991. The revolution began in 1987 when 300,000 gathered to protest in song. Now facing another kind of oppression, this time economic, 37,000 singers, musicians and dancers joined a six-hour-long parade in Tallinn. These music festivals, now held every five years, bring the nation together. Indeed, the festival is called, 'To Breathe as One'. Last year's festival drew a crowd of 200,000, and was watched on television by 1.3 million people, together almost half the population. The songs both bring the people together and generate a sense of national unity, thereby, creating a world.[76]

In her book *A Royal Waste of Time*, Marva Dawn tells the story of Vaclav Havel, a playwright who was also the president of the Czech Republic. He was asked how the revolution to overthrow communism in the Czech Republic was bloodless and yet had experienced real staying power. He simply replied, "We had our parallel society. And in that parallel society, we wrote our plays and sang our songs and read our poems, until we knew the truth so well that we could go out into the streets of Prague and say, 'We don't believe your lies any more!'" And communism had to fall. The songs created a parallel society that gave people a vision for their future. It's been said that, "You can make all the laws you want. Let me have a nation's music and I will rule that nation's hearts."[77]

And the songs we sing as Christians remind us of the different reality of which we are a part. They remind us of the truths of the gospel and therefore, implicitly, expose

76   ibid.
77   MJ Dawn, *A Royal Waste of Time: The Splendor of Worshiping God and Being the Church for the World*, Eerdmans, Grand Rapids, 1999, p. 334.

and undermine the lies of Satan and the world. Moreover, the songs we sing together reinforce our identity. When Christians of different backgrounds come together, there are certain songs that give us a sense of a common identity and heritage as we participate in singing them. Whether it is a favourite hymn like 'Amazing Grace' or 'And Can it Be', a much-loved children's song like 'Jesus Loves Me', a familiar Christmas carol like 'Silent Night', or a contemporary classic like 'Shout to the Lord', the songs express our common identity as citizens of the commonwealth of heaven.

7. Singing is communal

Connected with the above, singing is communal. As well as being an individual activity, it has always been something that communities have done together. That explains, in part, the perennial popularity of Christmas Carols by Candlelight gatherings. As the religious foundations of Christmas become a distant memory, and peoples' belief in, or even understanding of, the affirmations of the words of the carols grow increasingly weaker, they still love the experience of coming together as a community to sing with one voice songs familiar since childhood.

For Christians, congregational singing is one of the few things we do in church where we all actively participate. With the demise of the liturgy, prayers are now spoken entirely by an individual from the front (except in those churches where everyone speaks out loud together), and other communal activities such as the reciting of creeds are generally a thing of the past. But in song we all play a part. Of course, singing is also an individual activity but, in a sense, we forget our individuality when we join in congregational singing. In fact, one of the features of congregational singing is that no one voice dominates. Hymn writer, Brian Wren, says that, "We agree, in effect, not to be soloists, self-absorbed mediators, or competitors, but to compromise with each other, keep the same tempo, and thus love each other in the act of singing."[78]

When we sing as the assembled congregation we ought to hear the voice of the group, not one, two or three particular voices. Sadly, with the advent of the dominant song leader, whose voice is strengthened and magnified by the microphone, that communal dimension can be lost. The corporate voice of the congregation is muffled by the amplification. The song leader may think she is encouraging congregational participation by strong leading but, until the volume is lowered, her amplified voice overwhelms and smothers the community. It is impossible to compete with such volume and many, frankly, give up.

But when we sing communally we both affirm and express, in the midst of our diversity, our oneness as God's people. And, usually, this is done more effectively by singing than speaking. "Let's all say together the words of this psalm." Have you ever experienced the virtual chaos of a congregation trying to *say* together a psalm or a prayer or a speech? Some of us talk fast, some slow. Some take long pauses, others short. It's not easy to speak together in unison. But we can all sing together. The beat and time of the melody keeps us together. So, while we sing as individuals it is also a natural way for a community to express its common beliefs and longings.

78   B Wren, *Praying Twice: The Music and Words of Congregational Song*, Westminster John Knox Press, Louisville, 2000, p. 84.

8. Singing is commanded

To put it simply and bluntly, God commands his people to sing. The Old Testament contains literally hundreds of exhortations to God's people to sing to God, most of which are found in the book of Psalms. For example:

> Sing praises to the LORD, who sits enthroned in Zion!
>> Tell among the peoples his deeds! (Ps 9:11)

> Sing to God, sing praises to his name;
>> lift up a song to him who rides through the deserts;
> his name is the LORD;
>> exult before him! (Ps 68:4)

> Oh sing to the LORD a new song;
>> sing to the LORD, all the earth!
> Sing to the LORD, bless his name;
>> tell of his salvation from day to day. (Ps 96:1-2)

A wonderful example of this is the majestic Psalm 148. Here the song writer invites—indeed, commands—*all* of creation to sing to the Lord. Starting with all the heavenly hosts, he then catalogues each and every part of the created order. For all the differences between animate and inanimate objects, and for all the variety in the DNA makeup of a fish, a deer, or a human being, one thing unites them all: we were all made to praise the Lord.

As one preacher has colourfully expressed it, the song leader explores cosmology, meteorology, marine biology, geo-morphology, dendrology, zoology, ornithology, anthropology—and any other -ology that you care to mention—and exhorts them all to fulfil the purpose of their creation: to praise the Lord. And why? "For he commanded and they were created" (v. 5b).

Then the psalmist commands human beings, all 7 billion of us, from the greatest to the least to praise God. The song's climax calls upon the pinnacle of his creation, the righteous, the ones he delightfully describes as "the people close to his heart" (v. 14b, NIV), to praise him. Of course, as his people we are the ones who ought to be leading this cosmic choir in praise to God, not just because he has created us, but even more wonderfully because we know, and have experienced, his salvation through Jesus. He is the one who fulfils the promise of verse 14:

> He has raised up a horn for his people,
>   praise for all his saints.

The 'horn' is a popular biblical image for the victorious one who, by his power and strength, overcomes his enemies. Just imagine a large bull, with its head bowed, bearing down on its foe and then with his large, sharp horn tossing the creature like a rag doll over its head, to lie beaten and bloodied in the dirt. God's church has a horn, the Lord Jesus, who by his dying and rising won such a victory over sin, death and Satan, with a sharp stab into their hearts tossing them into death and defeat. So, we are commanded to praise the Lord.

Joining with all creation

There's a lovely reflection on Psalm 148 by the Lutheran poet and theologian, Gerhard Frost, that says:

We sat together,
this tall man and a tiny child,
before the fireplace.
Enthralled with this, her first,
and looking up at me,
She said,
"It's clapping!"

I would have said, "It's crackling,"
and so would you—
victims of the dulling years—
but who is right?
Who has really heard?
Can fire praise by crackling?

No, she's the one
who has found the word.
Indeed, it's clapping.
"Praise the Lord!"[79]

To put the sentiments of this poem more prosaically, how can we fail to see and appreciate that which the created order plainly recognizes: that the Lord God is worthy of all our praise? The One who is the joy of the earth and the heavens should all the more be the delight of men and women. Yet our praise is far richer than that of creation. Not only do we glorify the power of the Creator God, singing in the words of the classic hymn, "O Lord my God, when I in awesome wonder, consider all the works thy hands hath made", we also exalt him for his

79 GE Frost, 'Praise the Lord', in *Blessed is the Ordinary*, Winston Press, Minneapolis, 1980, p. 84.

redeeming grace: "And when I think that God, his Son not sparing, sent him to die, I scarce can take it in".[80] This expression of God's power and glory is not just something that impresses us from the outside, but something that has touched us deeply within. We are not just transfixed by the wonder of his creation, but we have been transformed by the power of his love and his work of new creation in our lives personally.

We have seen many compelling reasons for Christians to sing, not least of which is the command of God. Of course, God only commands that which is good for his people. That's why all the reasons we've outlined for why we should sing are, at the same time, aspects of the benefits of singing. Indeed, all we've seen in this chapter of the reasons for singing, are expressions of the virtues of this precious gift of God. Of course, singing is not the only way we praise God (a life of sacrificial obedience is an act of worship), but it accentuates our delight in God. Singing is not the only way we express our trust in God, but it enables us to express our faith with all our being. Singing is not the only way we express our communal identity as God's people, but the experience itself can be relationally enriching, and spiritually exhilarating.

So, let us sing.

80 Lines taken from verses 1 and 3 of 'How Great Thou Art'. The hymn was originally written in Swedish by CG Boberg in 1885. It was translated into English in 1949 by SK Hine, who added verses 3 and 4.

10

Where do emotions fit in?

Next to the Word of God, music deserves the highest praise. She is a mistress and governess of those human emotions... which control men or more often overwhelm them... Whether you wish to comfort the sad, to subdue frivolity, to encourage the despairing, to humble the proud, to calm the passionate or to appease those full of hate... what more effective means than music could you find?[81]

This is the reason why the prophets did not make use of any art except music; when setting forth their theology they did it not as geometry, not as arithmetic, not as astronomy, but as music, so that they

81 M Luther, 'Preface to Georg Rhau's *Symphoniae iucundae*' (1538) in J Pelikan and HT Lehmann (eds), *Luther's Works* (55 vols; trans. CM Jacobs; rev. EW Gritsch; Concordia/Fortress, Saint Louis/Philadelphia, 1955-86), vol. 53, p. 323.

held theology and music most tightly connected, and proclaimed truth through Psalms and songs.[82]

Those... who are not moved [by music] I believe are definitely like stumps and blocks of stone.[83]

Martin Luther

Scared of the song

In the introduction to this book, we told the story of Mike's surprising state of rapture at the playing of the 'Overture' from Puccini's opera, *William Tell*, at his son's school concert. One reader might respond, "Oh, I know just how you felt. That's why I love music and song; it's so exhilarating and exciting. I can almost forget my problems and my mundane existence and be transported to another world entirely. A wonderful world."

However, another reader might respond with a very different sentiment: "Yes, your testimony actually warns us why we need to be so careful with music. It is such a powerful medium that it can commandeer our fragile emotions, and take them to places they really ought not to go. We should be ruled by our heads not our hearts, and music circumvents the brain and seduces the heart. After all, how did the Pied Piper entice the children of the city of Hamlin to follow him to their graves? He played a

82   M Luther, 'Letter to Louis Senfl' (1530), *Luther's Works*, vol. 49, pp. 427-8.
83   ibid., p. 427.

mesmerizing, merry tune. Perhaps he played the *William Tell* 'Overture'!"

As the quotes above reveal, Martin Luther would have sympathized with the first of these responses, but not the second. He loved music and highly esteemed its affective powers. And yet the very thing that made Luther such an admirer of music—namely, its capacity to produce a variety of emotional dispositions—is precisely what has caused other Christian leaders to be far more restrained in their endorsement of music and song.

Reasons for reservations

Augustine's anxieties

The North African bishop, Augustine of Hippo (354-430), was one of the greatest theologians in church history, and his influence on Christian thinking continues down to today. In his famous work, *Confessions*, he extolled the value of Christian singing. He observed that when sacred words are combined with pleasant music, then "our souls are moved and are more religiously and with a warmer devotion kindled to piety than if they are not so sung".[84]

Augustine recognized and appreciated that when our emotions are moved by a song, the effect is not only felt in a warmer heart, but also expressed in an enhanced desire to please God, "a devotion kindled to piety".

At the same time, this great Church Father couldn't give singing his unqualified endorsement. He was too aware of the dangerous consequences of severing the

84   Augustine, *Confessions,* 9.6.14.

delight of the senses from the exercise of the mind. Therefore he warned:

> Yet when it happens to me that the music moves me more than the subject of the song, I confess myself to commit a sin deserving of punishment, and then I would prefer not to have heard the singer.[85]

Quite rightly, Augustine was concerned that the mind rule the heart, and that reason shepherd the emotions. He knew, presumably from experience, that at times believers can be so carried along by the music of the song that they are almost impervious to the words being sung.

And that happens all too often. Recently, Mike visited a church where they were singing the song 'Hear Us From Heaven'. Frankly, the words puzzled him:

> Lord, hear our cry, come heal our land.
> Breathe life into these dry and thirsty souls.
> Lord, hear our prayer, forgive our sin.
> And as we call on your name,
> Would you make this a place
> For your glory to dwell?
>
> *Chorus*
> Open the blind eyes. Unlock the deaf ears.
> Come to your people.
> As we draw near hear us from heaven.
> Touch our generation;
> We are your people, crying out in desperation.

85   ibid., 10.33.50.

Bridge (x4)
Hear us from heaven,
Hear us from heaven,
Hear us from heaven.[86]

To begin with, he wasn't sure whether the song was speaking about believers or unbelievers. Those to whom the song is addressed are described as blind and deaf—terms typically used to refer to unbelievers. On the other hand, the song asks God to come to his people as they draw near. This is clearly a reference to believers.

The lack of clarity only deepens when the song asks for God to "make this a place for your glory to dwell". Under the new covenant, the Lord resides in his people, not a particular place. Confused, Mike asked one of the church elders what he thought of the song (which, incidentally, was sung in endless repetition for around 10 minutes) meant. The elder admitted to him that he hadn't thought about it, *because he hadn't being paying any attention to the words!* He was so mesmerized by the melody that the fact that the words were actually incoherent and theologically confused had eluded him.

Perhaps we might say, since he wasn't really thinking about what he was singing, what harm was done? But that's precisely Augustine's concern. Music has the capacity to lull the senses, so that we stop thinking. And when the mind has begun to be disengaged in a Christian activity, then warning bells ought to start clanging. Just because the words of a song sound spiritual, does that mean we should close our eyes, lift our hands, enjoy the moment, and stop thinking? No way!

86   J Anderson, 'Hear Us From Heaven', 2006.

Calvin's concerns

Augustine is not the only important Christian thinker to raise concerns about the emotional power of music and song. The French-born Swiss pastor John Calvin was similarly qualified in his endorsement of singing. On the positive side, he readily acknowledged the value of singing the psalms (and also some of the Bible's other songs) because they "incite us to lift up our hearts to God and move us to an ardour in invoking and exalting with praises the glory of his Name".[87]

At the same time, Calvin had a very robust sense of the sinfulness of the human heart, and the propensity of fallen human beings to twist and pervert God's good gifts. He was thus aware of just how easily music can poison the mind, corrupt the heart, and, as a consequence, produce moral disaster. This is all the more so when it is married to falsehood. He therefore cautioned, "It is true that every bad word (as St Paul has said) perverts good manner, but when the melody is added, that word pierces the heart much more strongly and enters into it."[88] Calvin agreed with the ancient pagan philosopher Plato that when it comes to turning or bending our moral conduct this way and that, music is *the* most powerful force in the world.

Like Augustine, Calvin is careful to ensure that the sanctified head rules the regenerate heart, and so the

87   J Calvin, 'Articles for the Organization of the Church and its Worship at Geneva', 1537, in JKS Reid (ed.), *Calvin: Theological Treatises*, The Westminster Press, Philadelphia, 1954, p. 53.
88   J Calvin, 'Preface to the Genevan Psalter', 1565, in EA McKee (ed.), *John Calvin: Writings on Pastoral Piety*, trans. Charles Garside, Paulist Press, New York, 2001, p. 96.

words of a song rule the melody. Consequently, he placed a tight control on what was sung in his churches in Geneva. Only the words of Scripture. No secular melodies. No musical instruments.

Understanding emotions

The point underscored by this brief history lesson is that singing and music are so intimately connected to the emotional dimension of our personality, and so easily trigger powerful emotional responses, that we need to be discerning in our use of this force. In other words, Christian leaders like Augustine and Calvin aren't just a bunch of 'worship wowsers', or 'party poopers of praise'; their concerns are valid ones. Their desire is for the glory of God, the building up of the church, and the keeping of God's people from distraction and temptation.

So, where do we go from here? Surely, we don't want to conclude that music is a savage beast, and that the safest place for it is locked up in its cage? No. The Scriptures won't let us go there. So, we need to think about our emotions in a balanced and biblical way. Clearly, the Christian faith is based on facts not feelings; on what God has done for us objectively in the Lord Jesus, not upon how we happen to feel subjectively about it. But that understood, where do feelings fit in? Is it best to ignore them, or should we pay careful attention to them? Most importantly, how do we ensure that they are a help, rather than a hindrance, to godly Christian living and faithful Christian singing?

We don't intend to wade too deeply into the waters of the physiology of emotions, but we need to understand basically how they work. Robert Roberts, who has written extensively on emotions in the Christian life, calls them "concern-based construals".[89] What he means by this is that emotions—like joy, fear, anger, exasperation, regret—are the natural responses we have, when we grasp "with a kind of perceptual immediacy"[90] the significance of the situation we are in.

For example, when you're walking in the bush and you suddenly realize you are lost and night is approaching, you naturally experience a degree of fear. When you're told that your wife has just delivered a beautiful, healthy baby girl, and the significance of this event grips you, tears may fill your eyes, and joy flood your heart. By the same token, if you hear a talk about God's judgement on Sodom and Gomorrah and, by the work of the Spirit, realize that your position before the Lord is as perilous as was that of the people of Sodom, then the right emotional response will be one of terror.

When you sing the haunting words of Augustus Toplady's 'Rock of Ages'...

> While I draw this fleeting breath,
> When my eyelids close in death,
> When I soar through realms unknown,
> Bow before your judgement throne,
> Hide me then, my refuge be,
> Rock of Ages, cleft for me.[91]

---

89 RC Roberts, *Spiritual Emotions: A Psychology of Christian Virtues*, Eerdmans, Grand Rapids, 2007, p. 11ff.
90 ibid., p. 11.
91 A Toplady, 'Rock of Ages', 1763.

...then goose-bumps may rise on your arms and gratitude grip your heart because of all that the Saviour has done for you and the sure hope he has given you. In all of these cases, the response is both intellectual and emotional. Indeed, one would have to say that if it is not *both* intellectual *and* emotional, there is something profoundly wrong.

For while our emotional responses are largely involuntary, they are always influenced either by an instinct, a value, a belief or a thought. So, for example, if I'm told that the Australian cricket team has defeated England and regained the Ashes, my emotional reaction will depend on whether I'm English or Australian, whether I care about cricket, and whether I believe the news. In short, our emotions are never independent of our minds. At some level, they are always "concern-based".

Of course, how we express our emotional reactions will depend on a mixture of factors—for example, personality, upbringing, culture and context. So, for example, if you're told that a friend has just died, you may burst into tears or fall in a heap, or you may go very quiet, perhaps because that's how your family dealt with painful emotions or perhaps because you're in a crowded bus and don't feel at liberty to express your sadness.

Emotions, music and singing

Having made these general observations about emotions, our particular concern in this chapter is to understand the relationship between emotions, music and singing. To do this, it will help us first to think about music and emotions, before then turning to the difference that singing makes.[92]

Music and emotions

How do we begin to account for the fact that music can both express and arouse emotion? Stephen Davies, a philosopher at the University of Auckland, suggests that the connection lies in what he calls "appearance emotionalism".[93] That is, there is a connection between the appearance of something and the emotion it evokes. For example, we describe a willow tree as 'a weeping willow' because the tree is bent over, and so it appears to resemble a person racked with grief. Music, Davies argues, acts in much the same way. For example, by a gradual downward movement, or by employing dark timbres or thick harmonic bass textures, music can recall an appearance of sadness. Indeed it is well known that minor keys and slow tempos tend to express and evoke sadness, just as major keys and fast tempos tend to express and evoke happiness.

The fact that many listeners tend to have a similar response to the same piece of music suggests that there is some objective component to its emotional expressiveness. However, the words "tend to" must not be missed, for the reality is not all listeners have the same response to a piece of music (nor to a willow tree, for that matter). One person may be deeply moved by something they hear,

---

92 Much of what follows in this section is drawn from RS Smith, 'Music, Singing and Emotions: Exploring the Connections', *Themelios*, vol. 37, no. 3, 2012, pp. 465-79.

93 S Davies, 'Artistic Expression and the Hard Case of Pure Music', in M Kieren (ed.), *Contemporary Debates in Aesthetics and the Philosophy of Art*, Blackwell, Oxford, 2006, pp. 179-91.

while another quite unaffected. Each listener is therefore unique, and music is never heard in a vacuum.

Nonetheless, Luther was right about the power of music to enhance our emotional wellbeing. This has been confirmed by a number of neurological studies that have mapped the effects of music on those regions of the brain that are associated with our capacity to process and express emotion. What these studies show is that as these regions are stimulated by music, the effect is a highly therapeutic one for both mind and body. Dr Randall McClellan explains why:

> Emotions that are not expressed when they are felt may be turned inward where they can add stress to weakened parts of the body. When the stress is prolonged our natural ability to resist disease is impaired and illness may ensue... When used regularly, music is an effective vehicle for the dissipation of normal day-to-day emotional stress. But in times of intense emotional crisis, music can focus and guide emotional release by bringing the emotion to catharsis and providing it with the means of expression.[94]

Neurologist Oliver Sacks provides a deeply personal and moving account of the role that music played in lifting him out of depression after the death of his mother:

> For weeks I would get up, dress, drive to work, see my patients, try to present a normal appearance. But inside I was dead, as lifeless as a zombie. Then one

94   R McClellan, *The Healing Forces of Music: History, Theory, and Practice*, iUniverse.com, Lincoln, NE, 2000, p. 146.

day as I was walking down Bronx Park East, I felt a sudden lightening, a quickening of mood, a sudden whisper or intimation of life, of joy. Only then did I realize that I was hearing music, though so faintly it might have been no more than an image or memory. As I continued to walk, the music grew louder, until finally I came to its source, a radio pouring Schubert out of an open basement window. The music pierced me, releasing a cascade of images and feelings—memories of childhood, of summer holidays together and of my mother's fondness for Schubert... I found myself not only smiling for the first time in weeks, but laughing aloud—and alive once again.[95]

Singing and emotions

So, clearly, there is much to be said for the healing effects of music. But what happens when we bring the human voice into the picture? How does singing, in particular, both express and evoke emotion?

The human voice has the capacity to convey emotion in a range of different ways—through changes in pitch, contour, volume, etc. Not surprisingly, the six primary human emotions—fear, anger, joy, sadness, surprise, and disgust—are all usually expressed vocally, with strong acoustic variations. In other words, even if we don't understand the words someone is saying or singing—perhaps because they're speaking in a foreign language—it's usually fairly obvious what emotion is being conveyed.

95 O Sacks, *Musicophilia: Tales of Music and the Brain*, Picador, London, 2007, p. 298.

But here's the important thing: when we sing, we usually sing words with meanings, and those words not only express the *cognitive content* of the song, but the singing of them helps communicate the *emotional content* of the song as well. That is, the words convey both thoughts and feelings. Consequently, whenever we are hearing or singing a song, then emotions appropriate to the words are being stimulated.

This truth was captured beautifully and succinctly by the late Yip Harburg, the man who wrote the lyrics for all the songs in *The Wizard of Oz*, including the hauntingly evocative classic, 'Over the Rainbow'. What Harburg famously said was this: "Words make you think a thought; music makes you feel a feeling; a song makes you feel a thought".[96] The physiological reality behind this observation is that singing engages those parts of our brain (particularly in the right hemisphere) that speaking alone does not.

It's not surprising, then, that people who've experienced great trauma can sometimes find it very difficult to sing. Singing threatens to awaken their emotional processes, which have shut down in order to protect them from the full horror of what they have experienced. But it's also why singing can function as a very effective means of gently releasing suppressed emotions and of helping people to process the truth and reality behind their inner pain.

96 EY Harburg (1896-1981). The quote, which is ubiquitous on the internet, originally comes from a lecture given by Harburg at the New York YMCA in 1970.

Thinking theologically about emotions

Having offered these insights into our emotions from the world of physiology, we need to test them by Scripture. As with any topic, if we want to rightly understand the place and power of our emotions, it's essential to take our cues from the word of God, and not from the Siren voices of our culture. From the vantage point of the Bible we can say at least three important things about human emotions.

Part of our createdness

The first is that our emotions are part of the way God has made us. He has designed us to have feelings: to feel joy when things are good or disappointment when things are not. It's part of our being made in the image of God. For it is abundantly clear from Scripture that God himself is not only personal, rational and volitional, but emotional as well. He truly loves, indeed he is love (1 John 4:8)! His feelings, needless to say, are not of the same order as ours. We've already seen, to quote Spurgeon, that God rejoices "after a divine manner". This is true of all the divine emotions. But it's precisely because God is an emotional being that we who bear his image, and who have been made to reflect him and relate to him, are not only personal, rational, volitional and relational, but emotional as well.

In light of this, all we have seen in the previous section needs to be understood as God's gift. It is he who designed music as an inherently emotional medium, and it is he who has enabled us to 'feel a thought' by singing it!

Affected by our fallenness

Second, our emotional responses, and particularly the way we express them, are powerfully affected by our fallenness. What is true of every aspect of our humanity, is true of our emotions as well: we are by (fallen) nature sinners and, therefore, do not think, act or feel as we were made to. For, according to the Bible, our humanity has been corrupted and distorted at every level. Because of that, our emotional responses, which (as we've seen) are largely determined by our instincts, values, beliefs and thoughts, are in fact determined by *selfish* instincts, *corrupt* values, *false* beliefs and *foolish* thoughts.

For example, we often feel anger about things that don't anger God (like the weather) and, conversely, don't feel anger about things that do anger God (like greed and envy). Or, to make things even more complicated, we may have a right emotional reaction to a situation, but express it in a destructive or ungodly way, such as in an act of road rage! Or, the emotions we express, or don't express, may be out of all proportion to the event that has triggered them. For example, we might remain emotionally unmoved by a terrible human tragedy while being greatly depressed by the loss of a basketball game.

In short, because of sin, we are no longer emotionally straightforward. This, then, is the reason for Augustine's anxieties and Calvin's concerns with regard to music and song. These good gifts can be misused by us, particularly when they are used to cloud our minds or stir up an emotional reaction that is contrary to God's will. Or, worse, when they encourage us to 'feel a thought' that is either false or immoral.

Controlled by a renewed mind

Third, God's solution to the destructive impact of sin, and therefore the key to learning how to both experience and handle our emotions as we were meant to, and use music as we were meant to, begins with our being reborn by the work of God's word and Spirit. It likewise continues as our minds are renewed by God's word and Spirit. As Paul writes in Romans 12:2: "Do not be conformed to this world, but be transformed by the renewal of your mind".

As our minds are renewed by the work of God, so our instincts, values, beliefs and thoughts are conformed to the mind of God. As that happens, our emotional reactions and expressions are increasingly brought into line with the will of God. Now this, of course, is a lifelong and jagged process. Christian transformation moves forward one step at a time and, to be honest, sometimes it's 'two steps forward and one step back'. But God himself is committed to our transformation.

In summary, just as God's Spirit continually transforms our ways of thinking and patterns of behaviour, so he transforms our emotional responses as well. The greater our level of emotional maturity, the more wisely we will use music to evoke and express emotion. Conversely, the more wisely we use music, the more we will mature emotionally. Jeremy Begbie puts the point well: "To grow up into Christ is to grow up emotionally as much as anything else, and carefully chosen music in worship may have a larger part to play than we have yet imagined".[97]

97 JS Begbie, 'Faithful Feelings', in JS Begbie and SR Guthrie (eds), *Resonant Witness: Conversations Between Music and Theology*, Eerdmans, Grand Rapids, 2011, p. 353.

Remaining questions
Are we all meant to be the same?

All of this leaves us with a few remaining questions. First, are we all meant to be the same? Are we all emotionally wired in the same way? We've already seen that the answer to this question is 'No.' We are all different, and different by divine design. We have different personalities, we come from different families, and we've had different life experiences. More than that, cultures vary widely in their emotional responses. If we can generalize, Italians tend to be very emotionally expressive ('Mamma, mia!'), while those of an English background tend to be more emotionally reserved ('a stiff upper lip'). So it's very difficult, and not particularly helpful, to say that *this* is normal and *that* is not.

At the same time, one needs to avoid a relativizing and legitimizing of different cultural emotional responses. There are emotional extremes in any culture that need to be exposed and challenged. For example, there are people who are so emotionally volatile that they can become a danger, both to themselves and others. Conversely, there are people who are so emotionally frozen that they endanger their own emotional wellbeing, and impede their ability to emotionally engage with others. Therefore, some of us need help to harness our emotions, while others need help to release them. Even so, God is not seeking emotional uniformity, but emotional reality, tempered by other-person sensitivity. Therefore we have no need to be threatened by our differences.

What does this mean for our singing? While it is

impossible to divorce singing from emotions, what this will look like will vary from person to person. We have all been formed by our culture, family backgrounds and life experiences and these influences will inevitably shape how we express ourselves emotionally. In singing, some people are very expressive; they love to lift their hands, move their bodies, sing out loud, and glow with outward exuberance. Others are much more subdued in the way they sing, but their praise may be no less authentic. Moreover, we should never assume that the outward expression mirrors the inward reality. Therefore, we should beware of judging one another. Only God looks on the heart! Sadly, Rob knows of a church where if 'worshippers' don't lift their hands they're regarded as 'sub-spiritual'. This is tragic. Many whose emotional expressions are more visibly restrained, nonetheless have a deep love for the Lord Jesus, and an unquenchable joy in their salvation.

So we say it again: each of us is emotionally unique and all of us have a responsibility to express our emotions (either by reining them in or letting them out) in a way that best serves others.

What should we expect of our emotions?

The church gathering, then, should be a context for the good and helpful expression of our emotions. So often our own past experience of the expression of emotions in our gatherings shapes our thinking and practice. If you've been subjected to services where the use of music has been clearly manipulative—for example, where there are long periods of 'worship' where the type of song sung hardly engages the mind, people are encouraged to give little thought to those around them, and the emotions are used to produce an almost trancelike state—then you might be understandably wary of any singing that you perceive to be 'too emotional'. Conversely, if your church experience is so cerebral that music is marginalized and viewed with suspicion, and any display of emotion is seen as suspect and a mark of spiritual immaturity, then you may be frustrated that the service leaders are actually despising a good gift of God to his church.

What, then, should we expect of our emotions? We should expect them to be a normal part of our daily experience of being human and being alive. We will have emotional reactions of one kind or another, and we should thank God for them for they are part of the way he has made us. Given all we are taught both by Scripture and nature about the relationship between music and the mind, music and the emotions, music and the Spirit, we should expect singing to be an emotional activity. From that perspective, the anxiety some feel at even the slightest evidence of emotional engagement and enthusiasm in singing, to which we have just alluded, is perplexing. Indeed, Rob knows of another church where if a congregation member dares to lift their hands in praise, they can be sure to receive a 'pastoral visit'! This too is tragic. If you don't want water, don't turn on the tap. If you don't want emotions felt and expressed, don't start singing.

At the same time we must remember the Bible's teachings on the nature of men and women (created, fallen, and in the process of being renewed) and take heed of the wise cautions of some of our forebears in the faith. The relationship between congregational singing and emotions is not always healthy. As we've noted, it's possible to have a strong emotional response to words that may be banal or unbiblical. When this happens, the music has swayed the emotions, while the mind has exercised too little control. This is why it is important to remember that our emotions are not a reliable guide to the truth, and to ensure that our minds continually remain engaged that we might weigh what we are hearing or singing.

Having sounded these cautions, it's important to end this section on a positive note. For God wants us to not only 'think his thoughts after him', but to 'feel his feelings after him' as well—to share his passions, grieve his griefs and know his joys. This is part of our growth. Indeed it is part of the renewing of our minds. The great Jonathan Edwards saw this clearly. "There is a distinction to be made," wrote Edwards, "between a mere *notional understanding*, wherein the mind only beholds things in the exercise of a speculative faculty; and the *sense of the heart*, wherein the mind don't [*sic*] only *speculate* and *behold*, but *relishes* and *feels*."[98] So here again is where music and singing play a unique and vital role in the Christian life, and especially in our corporate gatherings. Why else do we usually sing after having listened to a sermon? It's not to stretch the legs or get the blood circulating, but to help us to marry together the cognitive and emotive dimensions of the truth of God's word.

After a sermon on the cross of Christ, for example, a wisely chosen song will both reinforce the truth of the

98   J Edwards, 'A Treatise Concerning Religious Affections', in E Hickman (ed.), *The Works of Jonathan Edwards*, Banner of Truth, Edinburgh, 1974, vol. 1, p. 283. Emphasis original.

message and enable the congregation to 'feel the thought' —that is, embrace this truth emotionally, and therefore more holistically. Indeed, over the years, Rob has often concluded his sermons, even some evangelistic ones, by singing a song himself before then leading people in prayer. Whilst we should always be alert to the risks of manipulation, we must not miss the many opportunities for creative edification. Let's avoid the dangers, but even more let's harness the benefits.

Conclusion: the head and the heart

It should be clear, then, from what we are saying that we do not believe that the head and the heart, the mind and the emotions are, in any way, at odds with each other. Our understanding of how God has wired us (our Biblical anthropology), and our own experience of the wonderful and harmonious blend of the intellectual life and the emotional life in others testify to the necessity of both godly thinking and godly feeling to mature Christian living. In writing on the psalms, John Piper puts it so well:

> We have been warned so often about not becoming a cold intellectual that we have trouble imagining the possibility of intellect that lights fires instead of putting them out. Or on the other side we have been taught to be so wary of fanatic emotionalism that we can scarcely believe that a tear in someone's eye might be coming from a holy syllogism instead of a pathological passion.
>
> God has given us minds and demanded that we

use them in understanding and applying his Word. And God has given us emotions which are equally essential and which he has commanded to be vigorously engaged in his service.

If we neglect the mind we will drift into all sorts of doctrinal error and dishonour God who wills to be known as he is. And if we neglect the heart we will be dead while we yet live, no matter how right our creed is. "This people honours me with their lips but their heart is far from me." So my goal for us is that we put together what so many keep apart to their own hurt. Let us be clear in our heads and warm in our hearts. Let us feel with all our might and think with all our might.[99]

When Christians think clearly with their minds and feel warmly in their hearts, they will love, they will trust, they will obey—and they will sing!

99   J Piper, 'Delighting in the Law of God', *Desiring God*, 21 July 1980 (viewed 28 July 2016): www.desiringgod.org/messages/delighting-in-the-law-of-god

11
Church music ministry: Where to from here?

Although there are things that can be done to enhance corporate worship, there is a profound sense in which excellent worship cannot be attained merely by pursuing excellent worship. In the same way that, according to Jesus, you cannot find yourself until you lose yourself, so also you cannot find excellent corporate worship until you stop trying to find excellent corporate worship and pursue God himself.[100]

DA Carson

The end of beginning

Well, we've just about reached the end of our exploration of the place and purpose of singing in the life of God's people. And we've covered a lot of territory along the way—virtually, the whole sweep of biblical history, and a

100 DA Carson, 'Worship Under the Word', in DA Carson (ed.), *Worship by the Book*, Zondervan, Grand Rapids, 2002, pp. 30-31.

good number of landmark moments in Christian history as well. But this is not really the end, not even the beginning of the end. It is, rather (to quote Winston Churchill), "the end of the beginning". For the church militant is destined to become the church triumphant; the pilgrim church, the glorified church. So there's a path of service ahead of us all, a path that will continue beyond life in this world, into the life of the world to come.

Our business in the present, then, is to grow toward the glorious future God has planned for us, to grow in Christlike character and to grow in our ability to use the gifts God has given us both for his glory and for each other's blessing. This, needless to say, includes the gifts of music and song.

Contemporary points of confusion

To that end, the aim of the first part of this chapter is to identify, and in the process seek to clear up, a number of points of confusion that regularly hamper effective church music ministry.

1. Confusion over the purpose of church

Many are confused about the purpose of church; that is, why we come together. Should we begin our time together by singing, "Here I am to worship" or "Here I am to edify"? Otherwise put, do we gather to meet God in the presence of one another, or do we gather to meet one another in the presence of God? As we've seen, the answer is both. We come to church to engage with God:

by hearing his word, confessing our sins, renewing our trust, singing his praise, offering up our prayers and so on. We likewise come together to engage with each other: by teaching, exhorting, rebuking, comforting, strengthening and encouraging one another. We do all of these things in the presence of God and we do all of these things in the presence of one another. Consequently, as we saw in chapter 6, our singing of psalms and hymns and spiritual songs is both *vertical* (we sing to the Lord) and *horizontal* (we sing to each other). So then, let us get beyond the needless either-or approach that has characterized so much in-house Christian debate, and let us strive to 'do church' in such a way that we truly serve one another to the glory of God, and sincerely draw near to God for the good of each other.

2. Confusion over the nature of worship

Many Christians are confused about the nature of worship. The New Testament is refreshingly clear that the worship that God desires and requires of his new covenant people embraces the whole person in all of life (Rom 12:1-2). God is not interested in compartmentalized worship (a.k.a. hypocrisy)! The great and first commandment remains the same: "You shall love the Lord your God with all your heart and with all your soul and with all your mind and with all your strength" (Mark 12:30).

Worship, then, is clearly not confined to Sunday, nor to church, and it's certainly not restricted to singing. Having said that, the 24/7 life of worship to which we are called clearly includes Sunday, embraces 'going to church' and finds expression in our singing. Indeed, it is still our bounden duty and great delight to "Serve the LORD with gladness" as we "come into his presence with singing!" (Ps 100:2)

So again, we need to get past an unnecessary and, in fact, unbiblical either-or approach to this question. Of course we come to church to worship God; it's just not the only way or time or place we are called to do that. Nor is worship the only way to describe the vertical focus of our gathering (e.g. we could use the language of honour, adore, glorify or magnify). 'Worship' is simply one biblical, historic and helpful umbrella term for our response to God, and 'corporate worship' a useful way of describing the Godward orientation of our gatherings.

But, as we've seen repeatedly, our gatherings have a one-another orientation as well. Rightly understood, the language of 'worship' or 'service' includes this dimension (see Rom 12:1-8; Acts 13:1-3). But the Bible also gives us a range of other ways to describe the purpose of our engagement with one another. So if we want to freshen up our language (or just give the language of 'worship' a rest), then we could express the purpose of our gatherings like this: *we come together both to glorify God and to edify one another*. Whatever words we settle on, it's a both-and!

3. Confusion over the purposes of singing

Confusion also abounds over the purposes of singing. Hopefully by now we've convinced you that we sing *both* to the Lord *and* to one another. But what does this mean in practice? Is our singing more a form of preaching or more a form of praise?

It is clear from Scripture that singing is a way of doing all manner of things. On the vertical front, it is a way of adoring, honouring, loving, thanking, glorifying, magnifying and exalting God. Indeed in singing, we are called to give ourselves wholeheartedly to God (e.g. Ps 138:1). But, of course, as we lose ourselves we find ourselves; in blessing we are blessed. That's why singing is regularly linked with exulting or rejoicing in God (e.g. Pss 5:11, 9:2, 68:4)! More than that, singing is also a way of praying to God, of confessing our sins to him, of expressing our pain and bewilderment and of interceding for others. Now, admittedly, singing is *not the only way* of doing any of these things, but it is certainly *one very biblical way* and *one very powerful way*—as it unites both heart and mind, and the whole congregation together, before the throne of grace.

On the horizontal front, singing is a way of teaching and admonishing, of exhorting and encouraging, of rebuking and comforting our brothers and sisters in Christ. It is even a way of evangelizing—of preaching the gospel to others and declaring the wonderful works of God to a lost and needy world. Instructively, many biblical depictions of praise cover both our singing to God and our singing to others. Indeed many passages weave them together in a deeply integrated way. For example:

Oh sing to the LORD a new song;
    sing to the LORD, all the earth!
Sing to the LORD, bless his name;
    tell of his salvation from day to day.
Declare his glory among the nations,
    his marvellous works among all the peoples!
For great is the LORD, and greatly to be praised;
    he is to be feared above all gods. (Ps 96:1-4)

So, once again, there is no need for us to choose. We sing to glorify God and to edify others; to thank him or pray to him *and* to instruct or preach to one another. And often (if not almost always) we do both at once.

4. Confusion over the power of singing

There is considerable confusion in the Christian world about the power God has given to music and song. For example, do our praises have the capacity to bring God closer to us? Can we 'sing down his presence', as some people have suggested?

What must be said, first up, is that while God clearly desires our praises, is honoured by them and can even, in some sense, be said to be enthroned on them (Ps 22:3), there is no hint in Scripture that they entice him to meet with us or arouse him to bless us. Biblical praise is always a *response* to the mercies of God, not a cause; it *celebrates* the gracious gift of his presence, rather than invokes it. In short, we initiate nothing! Consequently, songs that speak of *us* welcoming God into *our* presence are, frankly, verging on pagan!

So, if singing doesn't bring God closer to us, can it bring us closer to God? This is a different, more complex, question, requiring a two-part answer.

First, only Jesus Christ can bring us to God! So if, as a result of the Holy Spirit's work in us through the hearing of the gospel, we have come to put our trust in Christ, then we have already come to God and cannot come any closer. The New Testament makes this stunning point repeatedly (e.g. Rom 5:1-2; Eph 2:13, 3:11-12; 1 Pet 3:18; Heb 12:22-24). So, no, music can't bring us any closer to God, nor does it need to. Jesus Christ has done all that needs to be done—a liberating reality that can and should and will for eternity be celebrated in song.

However, there is more to be said. The New Testament is also clear that those who have been brought near to God through the blood of Christ need *continually* to "draw near" to him; that is, to *actualize* the benefits of Christ's saving work for us and *access* the present help he offers to us (Heb 4:16, 10:21-22). Now, again, this is something that God enables us to do. But we do it nonetheless.

But what does this have to do with music or singing? Potentially, quite a bit. Drawing near to God happens as we hear his word, put our trust in him, express our thanks and pray to him. What happens when we sing? We are (or, at least, should be) singing the word of Christ to one another (Col 3:16), expressing our faith in God and his grace, and (very often) giving him thanks and praying to him. That means singing is one of the ways we can draw near to God. Not surprisingly, as we've seen, Paul sees the singing of psalms and hymns and spiritual songs as one of the means by which God's children are filled by the Spirit with all the fullness of God (Eph 5:18-19; cf. Col 3:14-19). So, yes, in this sense singing can bring us closer to God, but not because it is singing— but because it is one way of hearing his word, trusting him, glorifying him and so on.

Perhaps an analogy might help. Imagine a married couple going out for a special celebratory dinner. Enjoying dinner together doesn't make them any more married, but it does provide them with a way of enriching and enjoying the relationship they have. In this sense, it brings them closer—not by creating something that isn't there, but by actualizing something that is there. In a similar way, when we who have already come to God through Jesus Christ faithfully sing the word of Christ, with thankful and prayerful hearts, so we are brought closer to him.

5. Confusion over the role of song leaders

There is widespread confusion over the role of song leaders. In fact, many churches are not quite sure what to call them—'worship leaders' or 'magnification ministers' or 'praise pastors'—and some are not sure whether to have them at all. Assuming we do have them (and in our judgement they are greatly beneficial), 'worship leaders' is a misleading descriptor, given that worship is much more than singing and singing is much more than worship. Even 'corporate worship leaders' is confusing, for our singers are not the only ones leading us in corporate worship of the Lord. 'Magnification ministers' seems a bit grandiose, 'music ministers' a bit formal and 'praise pastors' a bit restrictive (for they also lead us in preaching to each other). Our advice, then, is to stick with the accurate and the obvious: they lead us in song, so call them 'song leaders'.

But what is their precise role? Clearly, they do not (and must never try to) mediate God's presence to us. Rather, their job is *to help God's people glorify him together and edify one another*. But how should they do that? How prominent should they be? How strongly should they lead? How expressive should they be? How much should they speak? What should they wear?

The key to answering all such questions lies in properly understanding the job description above. Once this is grasped, all other questions can be worked out from there. For example, are the song leaders so loud that the congregation can't hear themselves and so have stopped singing? Or are the song leaders so quiet that the congregation lacks the direction and support they need to sing with confidence? Either way, there's a problem. For if the song leaders' task is to help the people of God sing to God and each other, then either they need turning up (if the congregation needs a stronger lead) or turning down (if it's being overwhelmed).[101]

Likewise, do the seraphic smiles and exuberant movements of the musicians help or hinder the congregation? Such questions can only be answered situationally; there is no 'one-size-fits-all' formula. Rob once visited a church where the musicians were concealed behind partitions so that the congregation couldn't see them. Perhaps this was necessary. Perhaps they were an easily distracted congregation? Usually, however, leadership requires visibility. Indeed, there is a place for song leaders to model an authentic engagement with God and others as they sing. However, the way this is done must always be tailored to the needs, culture, history and maturity of the people present.

Whatever the issue that needs resolving, the way forward is to seek to answer the question: *Is this hindering or*

101 In our experience, song leaders (and the church bands that accompany them) are often too loud. The congregation simply cannot compete with those who have the assistance of amplification, and so just give up. This is not because God is opposed to loud music. Quite the contrary (1 Chr 15:28; 2 Chr 20:19; Pss 33:3, 47:1, 150:5)! But if the song leaders and musicians have effectively silenced the congregation, then they have failed in their role. Their purpose is to assist and enable the congregation to sing to God and each other. If that's not happening because they're drowning out the congregation, then, like John the Baptist of old, they must decrease! Song leaders clearly need to be audible if they are to provide effective direction and support, but the main voices we should be aiming to hear during corporate singing are those of the gathered saints.

helping God's people to sing in such a way that God is glorified and the church edified?

6. Confusion over the place and value of emotional expression

As we've already seen, confusion over the place and value of emotions is nothing new. It's not our purpose here to repeat the arguments of the previous chapter. The main point that needs emphasizing and elaborating upon is the fact that Christians have shown themselves frighteningly prone to making a number of false equations. For example, for some, displays of emotionality are thought to be a sure sign that the Spirit is at work. For others, any expression of emotion in praise is thought to be an indication of immaturity or even self-centredness. Neither equation is necessarily correct.

No doubt, the Spirit of God can and does produce all kinds of emotional responses in us, but other things can do this as well (e.g. a bad night's sleep or carefully chosen music). Likewise, just as emotionality can be a sign of immaturity, so lack of emotion can be a sign of personal and spiritual deficiency. So it's best to refrain from making simplistic and uncharitable judgements.

As we said earlier, God is most interested in two things: *emotional authenticity* and *other-person sensitivity*. There is sometimes a tension between these two; for the first is about being honest, whereas the second is about putting the needs of others ahead of your own. However, they can also work happily together. For often what our brothers or sisters most need, is for us to be emotionally real, whether in joy or in grief. But where there is a conflict, then the clear call of Christ is to privilege the interests of others (Phil 2:4). That is the more excellent way!

This, of course, will not necessarily mean reining our emotions in—although sometimes that may be what's required. It might well mean letting our emotions out—even when that doesn't come easily to us. This alerts us to yet another possible false equation: that the best way to truly serve others is by damping down our emotions so they won't feel uncomfortable. Who says? Perhaps the best thing we can do for another is to discomfort them; perhaps to challenge them out of their complacency? Of course, rather than feeling uncomfortable, they might be profoundly encouraged by seeing you give yourself to the praise of God, with mind and heart and body, even though you're dog-tired or battling a cold!

It's vital that we move past being children in our thinking about these matters. Those of us in Christian leadership have a responsibility to talk about them, teach about them and urge God's people toward both genuine emotional expressiveness and genuine other-person-centredness in their singing of God's praise and God's word. Doubtless, we would also do well to encourage a 'unity in diversity' culture with regard to the way that people express themselves. We have not been designed to be emotional clones of each another, and so should not be threatened or divided by our emotional differences.

Perennial points of tensions

Having addressed some points of current confusion, we now turn to some of the more perennial sources of tension that many churches, and many church musicians, have to learn to either resolve or manage.

1. Singing scriptural words versus singing scriptural truth

There has been a long-standing and sometimes heated discussion—going right back to the early church and continuing to the present day!—as to whether God's people should only sing Scripture or whether we are also free to sing songs of "mere human composure" (to use an expression from the 1673 'Preface' to the *Scottish Metrical Psalter*).

As we've already made mention, the hymns of Isaac Watts caused considerable controversy in the 18th century, disturbing many believers and dividing many churches. In England, for example, one opponent expressed great concern to see "Christian congregations shut out divinely inspired Psalms, and take in Watts' flights of fancy; as if the words of a poet were better than the words of prophet, or as if the wit of a man was to be preferred to the wisdom of God".[102] In America, the Rev. Adam Rankin rode his horse all the way from Kentucky to Philadelphia to beg the General Assembly of the Presbyterian Church "to refuse the great and pernicious error of adopting the use of Isaac Watts' hymns in public worship in preference to the Psalms of David".[103] So this is a question that has aroused strongly felt passions.

102 W Romaine, 'An Essay on Psalmody', in *The Whole Works of the Late Reverend William Romaine A.M.*, Thomas Tegg & Son, London, 1837, p. 990.
103 Cited in RJ Morgan, *Then Sings My Soul: 150 of the World's Greatest Hymn Stories*, Thomas Nelson, Nashville, 2003, p. 35.

And, in one sense, so it should! Nothing is more important than the will of God and, when it comes to church music, nothing is more important than singing the word of God. The question, however, is whether the word of God can only be sung in the form of direct scriptural quotation. The answer to this should be fairly obvious. For if the answer were "Yes", then preaching the word of God should (by the same logic) be reduced to Bible reading. But, as far as the New Testament is concerned, this is not the case; the "public reading of Scripture" and "preaching and teaching" are different activities (1 Tim 4:13, NIV). So then, just as the word of God can be spoken in words other than direct scriptural quotation, so it can also be sung in words other than direct scriptural quotation. Indeed, as we saw in chapter 6, Paul's references to the singing of "psalms and hymns and spiritual songs" refer to more than the book of Psalms. God, then, has not bound us to sing only from the Old Testament Psalter.

Having said that, we wholeheartedly agree with Dietrich Bonhoeffer that "whenever the Psalter is abandoned, an incomparable treasure vanishes from the Christian church".[104] For the psalms are not only human words to God but (unlike songs of "mere human composure") God's words to us! More than that, they contain, as John Calvin memorably put it: "An Anatomy of all Parts of the Soul; for there is not an emotion of which any one can be conscious that it is not represented here as a

104 Bonhoeffer, *Psalms*, p. 26.

mirror."[105] The psalms, then, teach us to praise God and to pray to him both in a truly human way and in divinely inspired words. So it will only be to our great gain to work out how to make good use of them both personally and corporately.

But the psalms are not the only songs in the Bible, nor must we only sing 'straight Scripture'. Our calling is to sing "the word of Christ" (Col 3:16); that is, the truth of the gospel. The key to faithfully singing this word, like the key to preaching it, is *the clear communication of the meaning of Scripture*—whether in direct scriptural language or in the words of "human composure".

2. Preserving the past versus connecting with the present

Every church has a history. Every church has its traditions. Our past is important, for we haven't come from nowhere, and our traditions, oftentimes, have not only served us well, but are greatly valued by older members of our congregations. At the same time, every church exists in the here and now and so has a responsibility to serve its present members and bear witness to the world around it. Consequently, these two influences—the historic and the contemporary—compete, and often fight, with one another. This is one of the reasons for the long history of (so called) 'worship wars'!

Nevertheless, these two streams of influence actually

---

105   J Calvin, 'The Author's Preface', in *A Commentary on the Book of Psalms*, translated from the original Latin and collated with the author's French version by J Anderson, vol. 1, Christian Classics Ethereal Library, Grand Rapids (viewed 28 July 2016): www.ccel.org/ccel/calvin/calcom08.vi.html

need each other desperately. The contemporary protects the historic from the idol of traditionalism (or mindless custom) and the historic preserves the contemporary from the folly of eccentricism (or needless novelty). So, the tension produced by the intersection of the past and the present is a necessary and healthy one. Consequently, the best way to manage it is to allow them both to continually interact with each other, challenging, correcting and supplementing each other as they inevitably do.

Musically, this interactive process usually produces some form of what is often called 'blended worship'. That is, a combination (ideally, of the 'best bits') of the past and the present, the historic and the contemporary, the old and the new. Such an outcome not only avoids having to pick sides in the 'war', but is an acknowledgement of the fact that "all things are yours" in Christ (1 Cor 3:21), and that we are free to make good use of all the gifts and resources available to us.

What's more, if Scripture is our guide, there is no single divinely sanctioned song form or poetic genre, nor does God have a preferred musical style or favourite set of musical instruments. So, as we sing both to God and to each other, our aim should be to do all things "for the glory of God" (1 Cor 10:31, NIV) and "so that the church may be built up" (1 Cor 14:26, NIV), and "in a fitting and orderly way" (1 Cor 14:40, NIV). If we keep that threefold aim in focus, it is usually not too difficult to work out the best 'blend' (which will, no doubt, be partly determined by context, demographics, personnel and resources) of biblical psalms, historic hymns, contemporary songs, musical styles and musical instruments.

3. Countering culture versus capturing culture

Another longstanding debate (again going back to the early centuries) is over whether Christians should be free to make use of the various musical genres or styles of the cultures that surround us (effectively taking them captive for Christ), or whether we should aim to be 'counter-cultural', even developing our own distinctively Christian musical style. In wrestling with this tension, three things need to be kept in mind.

First, no musical style is evil in itself. The ability to make music is one of God's good gifts to the human race, and he has given us the creative capacities to craft all kinds of instruments and develop a plethora of diverse musical styles. Whilst most of us will inevitably like some of these styles more than others—usually for reasons of familiarity—that is most often a matter of our subjective tastes rather than a reflection of their objective value. We should be very wary, then, of 'sanctifying' our personal preferences, as if God was only in favour of (say) Celtic music or 'high culture art' and had no time for Latin music or 'pop culture art'. Like our facility to speak languages, our tastes will be limited, but God's are not. All things are ours—even if we don't or can't make use of them all!

Second, any and every musical style can be used destructively or for idolatrous purposes. It's a matter of both intent and consequence, and ultimately an issue of (what we might call) 'worship direction'. In short, is the music being used in the service of God or an idol? Is the effect of this type of song edifying or unedifying? Now, here's where things can get messy. For whilst no musical genre is evil in itself, at certain times and places a particular musical genre can become so entangled with an idolatrous aspect of culture that it becomes very difficult (if not impossible) for Christians to make use of it.[106] Likewise, certain musical styles don't work well for certain cultures or demographics (e.g. highly syncopated rhythms for those over 70). This shouldn't trouble us, for there are always lots of other musical options to explore and make use of. Also, the good news is that often over time a 'tainted genre' can disentangle itself from the cultural idolatry that once enslaved it and so be 'recaptured for Christ'!

Third, because not all musical genres do the same 'job', invariably some will be more conducive to singing the word of Christ than others. If the purpose of congregational songs is to convey scriptural truth with clarity, then musical styles that make that more difficult, perhaps because they're too busy or complicated, or perhaps because they prioritize the emotional affect of the music over the cognitive content of the words, will be less helpful for teaching and admonishing one another. Obviously, there are personal and cultural elements involved in such judgements, so again there is no 'one-size-fits-all' approach. If we have the right target in focus—i.e. singing

---

106 For example, when rock 'n' roll first emerged in the 1950s, it was strongly linked with teenage rebellion and the overthrow of traditional authorities, beliefs and morality. As Steve Turner has written: "Rock 'n' roll was the sound of a generation slipping free from the restraints of the past" (S Turner, *The Gospel According to the Beatles*, Westminster John Knox Press, Louisville, 2006, p. 58). It would take some time for these associations to fade and for Christians to be able to use it safely and without risk of syncretistic compromise. So whilst Larry Norman was right to sing, "Why should the devil have all the good music?" (in the song of that title on his 1972 album, *Only Visiting this Planet*), the fact is that when a particular genre becomes linked to a form of cultural idolatry, much patience and wisdom are required in capturing it for the cause of Christ.

scriptural truth with clarity—then, whatever our culture, our situation or the demographics of our congregation, we'll be in a good place to make appropriate judgements about what musical genres best serve that end.

4. Lyrical substance versus musical form

It ought now to be clear that the *lyrical substance* of our congregational songs is of the utmost importance. No matter how good a tune might be it can never substitute for a lack of biblical content or gospel clarity. However, it is also true that putting an inappropriate or ill-fitting tune to solid biblical words is bound to severely limit their usefulness, if not render them ineffectual. So, if our aim is to sing the word of Christ faithfully and with the greatest edificatory effect, then we will be concerned not only for *faithful lyrical substance* but also *effective musical form*. What will this mean in practice? What kinds of questions might it force us to ask?

Here are some of the more obvious ones: Do the words and music work well together? Does the mood of the music suit the mood of the words, or is there a clash between the two? Does the tempo of the music allow the content of the song to be grasped and communicated, or is the message being lost? Is the music so irregular and counterintuitive that most of our energies are absorbed by the effort to follow where the melody is going, leaving little left to meditate on the message or meaningfully sing it to others? Is there a satisfying match between the melodic and musical highs and lows and the lyrical progression and resolution? Or are they working against each other at points?

Ideally, these are the kinds of questions that should be being asked by those who write our congregational songs (and, of course, often they are!). But they are also questions for those who choose them or who are (perhaps) looking for the best tune to put with the words of the hymn. This is why some, like Rob, have taken up the task of writing fresh tunes to a number of older hymns. We not only need the words to communicate clearly but also the music to communicate effectively, and for the two to work together in harmony!

As we've already seen, there is an unavoidable cultural and subjective component to our judgements in this area. So the best choice in one context may not be the best choice in another. There is likewise a 'communal component' that needs to be appreciated and can only be discovered by feedback from the congregation. For instance, is the song too high for *this* congregation? Is it enabling *them* to sing God's praise to his glory and his word to each other? We should not presuppose the answers to these questions, or assume that just because a song works well in the church down the road it will work well in yours!

5. Corporate versus individual

In case we hadn't noticed, every church is made up of individuals. But we are not isolated individuals. Rather, we are profoundly united: united by the same Spirit, united as members of the one body of Christ, united as children of the same heavenly Father! This, indeed, is one of the chief things that draws us together: we belong together and so gather to meet Christ in each other and serve one another with the gifts we've each been given for the common good (1 Cor 12:7).

All of this has profound implications for congregational singing. At the risk of repetition, not only do we together sing 'up' to glorify the Lord, who is our primary audience, but we together sing 'around' to edify each other, the secondary audience. What's more, our singing is both a way of fostering our unity in Christ, as it is a way of giving praise and thanks God. Little wonder that Paul was moved to pray: "May the God of endurance and encouragement grant you to live in such harmony with one another, in accord with Christ Jesus, that together you may with one voice glorify the God and Father of our Lord Jesus Christ" (Rom 15:5-6).

But does this concern for unity mean that churches should only sing in the 'first person plural', and never in the 'first person singular'? That is, should we only sing 'we songs', not 'I songs'? There is certainly a strong argument for singing lots of 'we songs' together. They remind us of the reality of our unity, expressing and reinforcing this truth in a clear and powerful way. They also provide a healthy check on our innate individualism, if not a gentle challenge to our ingrained tendency to think primarily of *our*selves, *our* needs and *our* worship—even when we come together.

However, if the book of Psalms is any guide, there is also an important place for a good number of 'I songs'.[107]

---

107 It is important to realize that the book of Psalms is not, in the first instance, a book about either the individual believer's or the community's life of faith. Its substance and shape reflect the historic progression of Davidic kingship in light of the promise made to the Lord's anointed (Ps 2:7; cf. 2 Samuel 7). What this means is that the 'I' of the psalms is very often the 'I' of the king, the Messiah, and so, in the fullness of time, of great David's greater son, Jesus Christ. Therefore, as Dietrich Bonhoeffer rightly saw, if we want to read, pray or sing the psalms, "we must not ask first what they have to do with us, but what they have to do with Jesus Christ" (Bonhoeffer, *Psalms*, p. 14). However, even in the Old Testament, God's Messiah is never to be thought about independently of "all who take refuge in him" (Ps 2:12). For new covenant believers our relationship is even more profound; we are 'in Christ'. This means we have every reason to make Jesus' psalms ours, particularly as we sing them back to him in prayer or in praise.

For such songs express and encourage a profound personal ownership of the truths we sing. They call us to trust or give thanks or dedicate ourselves afresh (or, perhaps, for the first time) to the God whose glory and gospel we declare in our praise. What's more, as AW Tozer points out, 'I songs' are not, in fact, the enemy of *corporate* singing:

> Someone may fear that we are magnifying private religion out of all proportion, that the "us" of the New Testament is being displaced by a selfish "I." Has it ever occurred to you that one hundred pianos all tuned to the same fork are automatically tuned to each other? They are of one accord by being tuned, not to each other, but to another standard to which one must individually bow. So one hundred worshippers meeting together, each one looking away to Christ, are in heart nearer to each other than they could possibly be were they to become "unity" conscious and turn their eyes away from God to strive for closer fellowship. Social religion is perfected when private religion is purified. The body becomes stronger as its members become healthier. The whole church of God gains when the members that compose it begin to seek a better and a higher life.[108]

In short, what really matters is that we praise God *personally in* the congregation and praise him *corporately as* the congregation. Whether we do that with singular or plural pronouns is simply a matter of verbal form, not of

108 AW Tozer, *The Pursuit of God*, Christian Publications, Camp Hill, 1982, p. 65.

theological substance or ecclesiological reality. Nevertheless, for the reasons given above, usually an even mixture of 'I' and 'we' songs will be helpful.

6. Participation versus performance

We come finally to the tension between participation and performance. Is there a place for being sung to, as well as singing together? And, if so, what is that place?

Before we come to that question, it may first help us to address the broader issue of 'performance' and its place in Christian gatherings. 'Performance' is something of a dirty word in many churches. There's sometimes a good reason for this. Too many of us have encountered the church 'performer' (perhaps in ourselves!) who is motivated more by a need for admiration and adoration, than by a desire to assist God's people in glorifying him and edifying each other. So let's be clear: song leaders are not entertainers and the congregation is not a concert crowd. The congregation is the choir, the song leaders and musicians are the accompanists, and God is the ultimate audience.

Once we've got that clear, and provided we keep it clear, it is important to distinguish between appropriate and inappropriate 'performance'. For there's nothing inherently wrong with the idea of performance. Anyone who does anything in church, from the ushers to the preacher, is performing a task. They can either perform their task humbly and helpfully, or perform it badly. So what makes the difference? As we saw in our discussion of musical styles, the keys are *intent* and *consequence*. That is, is the task performed with God-glorifying intent and with other-edifying effect?

But what determines edifying effect? The answer, at least from the human side, is *understanding* and *skill*. It takes understanding to know what to do and skill to do it well. Having spent most of this book exploring the understanding side of things, let's consider the importance of skill, particularly as it relates to music.

It takes most people about 10,000 hours of practice to learn to play an instrument competently. Learning to play in a way that helps others to sing easily and effectively is often an additional skill. Therefore, to perform their task well, church musicians need to have invested a considerable amount of time in skill development. And if they have developed such skills, then Scripture exhorts them not to hide them, but to employ them to the greatest effect (Ps 33:1-3)! Herein lies the benefit of rescuing the word performance, provided we are clear about the difference between appropriate and inappropriate 'performance' when it comes to church music.

So, to come back to our initial question: Is there a place for being sung to in church? Once again, if Scripture is our guide, the answer is a very definite 'Yes'. For if the word of Christ can be taught or read to us by one person, it can clearly be sung to us by one person. Not surprisingly, the psalms contain numerous references to individuals singing in the midst of the congregation (e.g. Pss 22:22, 25; 35:18; 111:1). The apostle Paul likewise envisages the same phenomenon in the new covenant church (1 Cor 14:26). Moreover, not only did the Israelites have a choir who led them in praise, as we saw in chapter 3, but numerous psalms are addressed "To the choirmaster", indicating that some psalms were sung (if not in whole, at least in part) by the choir to the congregation. So we have numerous biblical precedents for 'special music' or 'choral items' or 'solos' in church.

However, what is regrettable, in our judgement, is when congregations are sung to more than they sing themselves. As we've seen, Paul's exhortations are all-inclusive: we are to glorify God with one united voice as we all address one another in psalms and hymns and spiritual songs. What's more, the picture in Revelation is of "every creature in heaven and on earth and under the earth and in the sea, and all that is in them" singing praises to God and the Lamb (Rev 5:13). When it comes to church music, then, congregational singing should be the 'main game,' that we might learn to reflect the songs of heaven in this world and prepare ourselves for praises of the world to come.

So let's work at getting the balance right between the singing of some and the singing of all, understanding that the song of the one (which clearly has its place) is intended to lead to the song of the many. No doubt, this is why David's determination to personally "bless the LORD at all times" (Ps 34:1), is followed immediately by his passionate invitation: "Oh, magnify the LORD with me, and let us exalt his name together!" (v. 3)

The beginning of the end

Both Mike and Rob have a dream! It's the dream that has driven us to write this book. We long to see those who have been saved by the blood of Christ recover the vital place of congregational singing in the life of his church, and rediscover the powerful God-given purposes that singing is designed to accomplish in our gatherings. Otherwise put, we long to see churches glorifying God by singing his praise and edifying each other by singing his word, and doing so with minds, hearts and bodies engaged in faith, hope and love.

Of course, this dream will one day become reality—of that we have no doubt! For on the day when Jesus comes again in glory, raises the dead, judges the world and consummates his Father's kingdom, there will be no more hindrances or obstacles to our praise of the triune God. Indeed, as we find ourselves at 'the beginning of the end'— the end for which we were created—we shall leap like calves from the stall into an eternity of uninhibited worship (Mal 4:2; Rev 22:3) and take our part in that "Great Story which no-one on earth has read: which goes on for ever: in which every chapter is better than the one before".[109]

But we don't have to wait until then! Even now we can grow in our willingness and ability to serve the Lord, his people and his purposes in our singing. Indeed, our hope and prayer in writing this book is that we might all be inspired and enabled to make genuine progress in praise as we move toward that glorious day when "the earth shall be full of the knowledge of the LORD as the waters cover the sea" (Isa 11:9). So, come, let us be about our musical business in this world; "let us sing to the LORD; let us make a joyful noise to the rock of our salvation!" (Ps 95:1).

109 CS Lewis, *The Last Battle*, HarperCollins, London, 1990, p. 172.

 **matthias**media

Matthias Media is an evangelical publishing ministry that seeks to persuade all Christians of the truth of God's purposes in Jesus Christ as revealed in the Bible, and equip them with high-quality resources, so that by the work of the Holy Spirit they will:

- abandon their lives to the honour and service of Christ in daily holiness and decision-making
- pray constantly in Christ's name for the fruitfulness and growth of his gospel
- speak the Bible's life-changing word whenever and however they can—in the home, in the world and in the fellowship of his people.

Our resources range from Bible studies and books through to training courses, audio sermons and children's Sunday School material. To find out more, and to access samples and free downloads, visit our website:

www.matthiasmedia.com

How to buy our resources

1. Direct from us over the internet:
   – in the US: www.matthiasmedia.com
   – in Australia: www.matthiasmedia.com.au

2. Direct from us by phone: please visit our website for current phone contact information.

3. Through a range of outlets in various parts of the world. Visit **www.matthiasmedia.com/contact** for details about recommended retailers in your part of the world.

4. Trade enquiries can be addressed to:
   – in the US and Canada: sales@matthiasmedia.com
   – in Australia and the rest of the world: sales@matthiasmedia.com.au

---

Register at our website for our **free** regular email update to receive information about the latest new resources, **exclusive special offers**, and free articles to help you grow in your Christian life and ministry.

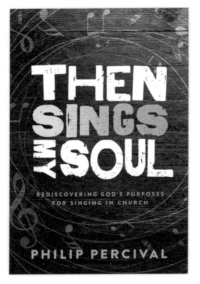

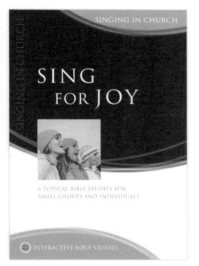